IDEA MAKERS

15

FEARLESS FEMALE ENTREPRENEURS

LOWEY BUNDY SICHOL

WOMEN OF POWER

CHICAGO REVIEW PRESS

T0062675

Copyright © 2022 by Lowey Bundy Sichol
All rights reserved.
First hardcover edition published in 2022
First paperback edition published in 2024
Published by Chicago Review Press Incorporated
814 North Franklin Street
Chicago, Illinois 60610
ISBN 979-8-89068-002-0

The Library of Congress has cataloged the hardcover edition
under the following Control Number: 2021948296

Cover, illustrations, and interior design: Sadie Teper

Printed in the United States of America

For Carter, Peyton, and Tucker

Be Fearless.

Contents

Introduction

Have you ever thought, *I wish someone made [insert idea here]*?
Or have you ever realized, *I have a great idea for [insert idea here]*?
Or have you ever seen a new product and exclaimed, *I could have
invented that!*

If your creative mind thinks this way, then you have the seeds of
becoming an entrepreneur, a founder of a business. Today, there are
more female entrepreneurs in the world than ever before: 12.9 million businesses are run by women in the United States, making up
approximately 40 percent of all the companies in the United States.
Together, these women-run businesses generate $1.9 trillion in sales
each year! Also exciting is that 50 percent of women-operated businesses in 2019 were founded by women of color, and this number is
increasing by about 7 percent each year.

But why do we rarely hear there their stories? And how can *you*
start a business with *your* idea? This book was written to inspire kids
to be the world's next great entrepreneurs and business leaders. By
reading the stories of how other people did it, you will learn how to

do it yourself. (That's also how the best business schools in the world teach entrepreneurship.)

Idea Makers: 15 Fearless Female Entrepreneurs is all about how 15 women turned their ideas into some of the biggest and most successful companies in the world. This book features female entrepreneurs in five industries: food, health and beauty, science and technology, education, and clothing and fashion. In each story, you'll find common threads linking each of these women.

First, when each female founder was a young girl, she showed hints of what she was both good at and passionate about. For example, Anne Wojcicki loved biology throughout school, and Christina Tosi enjoyed baking for friends and family. These precocious interests would prove to be very important later in life.

Second, each female founder gained valuable experience at her first job, learning skills that would later help her run her business. For example, Alli Webb worked at a salon blowing out and styling hair, and Cindy Mi taught kids in China how to speak English.

Third, each female founder had a moment in her life when her idea really came to fruition. Sometimes it happened slowly over the course of several years, like Jasmine Crowe's desire to feed hungry people. Sometimes it came out of survival like Kathleen King, who reinvented her cookie business after a bad partnership. And sometimes it hit like a bolt of lightning, like how Sara Blakely had her idea for a new type of undergarment for women while getting dressed for a party. But one thing they all had in common—once that idea was in their heads, nothing could stop them and they all dove into the world of entrepreneurship.

Together, these 15 women are worth billions of dollars, employ tens of thousands of individuals, and have gone on to change the world. Now, it's your turn.

Part I: Food

Kathleen King: Tate's Bake Shop

Kathleen walked into the vacant bakery. Two other bakeries had rented the space before, the landlord explained, and the air still smelled like flour. The kitchen was fully equipped with professional baking equipment and a large refrigerator. The space wasn't huge, but significantly bigger than her mother's kitchen at the farmhouse where she had baked her cookies for almost a decade. And the quaint storefront would be perfect to display and sell her baked goods. There was even a cash register in place.

"I wonder why the other bakeries failed," Kathleen's mother wondered.

"Well, it's obvious," Kathleen explained confidently. "They didn't have cookies as good mine."

Kathleen King was born on December 18, 1958. Her parents, Millie and Richard "Tate" King worked tirelessly to support their four children: Richie, Karin, Kevin, and Kathleen. Millie stood tall at five foot eight and was a registered nurse at Southampton Hospital, which brought in a meager but steady income. Her work schedule was anything but steady, however. Sometimes Millie worked the morning shift, which meant she had to arrive at work before the children woke up. And sometimes she worked the night shift, which meant she was gone the entire evening. As a result, Kathleen learned to be independent at a young age.

Tate, on the other hand, was a very short man, only five feet tall, about the height of an average seventh grader. But his short stature never held him back. He ran North Sea Farm, the family farm that included 15 acres of farmland, approximately 24 cows, and over 2,000 chickens. Tate sold milk to a local dairy and sold eggs to residents, restaurants, and grocery stores in Southampton, New York. Everyone knew and adored Tate King, who worked extremely hard, loved his community, and rarely left the farm. He often told his children, "We're the richest family in town because we're richest in family, friends, and spirit."

Despite laboring day and night to make ends meet, the King family did not have much money. They didn't go on vacations and never ate in restaurants. Sometimes, money was so tight that Tate would barter or trade animals from the farm for products or services his family needed. Once, he bartered half a steer to secure dentist appointments for his children.

But lack of money didn't stop Millie and Tate from being extremely generous with their time and resources. Tate loved to help his neighbors with odd jobs that needed attention. He believed if you had two apples, you sold one and gave the other away. "I've always told my kids to go out of your way for other people and help them every way you

3

can," Tate once told Kathleen. "If you can get along with people and you've got ambition, you've got it 95 percent made."

Mille and Tate King raised their four children to be fiercely independent with more responsibilities than most adults. They parented by this philosophy: "If you can walk, you can work." Everyone pitched in and helped both in the house and on the farm, regardless of gender or age. "I had a mother who was ahead of her time," Kathleen recalls. "It was all about the work that needed to be done before the day was over, inside and outside the house. . . . By the time I was 11, I could already make dinner, clean the house, do the laundry, work the farm, and wait on customers."

Growing up on the farm, Kathleen considered herself to be an average kid. She wasn't the smartest student in the class and often struggled with her schoolwork. She wasn't popular among the kids and felt more comfortable at the farm with her family. And she wasn't particularly athletic, either. But Kathleen was a tough kid with a great work ethic. "I was also a tomboy," Kathleen says. "Always dirty, always keeping up with everyone else on the farm. I firmly believed that if *you* could lift it, *I* could lift it."

Kathleen's First Job

During the summer of 1969, Kathleen was 11 years old and busy with her regular chores around the house and farm. Her father approached her one breezy evening in early June. Visitors were starting to return to Southampton for summer vacation, and farm stand sales were picking up.

Tate needed extra help at the farm stand, and Kathleen's older siblings had already gotten summer jobs in town. So, he turned to Kathleen. Tate explained that Kathleen would "take over the business." That meant she would run the farm stand and bake cookies for it, to help generate some extra sales. Tate's rules were clear. He would provide all the ingredients, including fresh eggs from the family farm, and Kathleen would keep all the profits from her cookie sales. In return, Kathleen would use her profits to buy her clothes for school in the fall.

It seemed like a fair deal, and Kathleen immediately responded, "Yes, Daddy."

Kathleen's Tip: Kids can do more than their parents think. Even as young as age seven or eight, children can learn from their parents how to handle a knife, how to turn on the stove, how to put things in the oven, and how to cook dinner.

The next morning, Kathleen woke up ready to bake cookies. She gathered the ingredients from her mother's kitchen and turned to the only chocolate cookie recipe she knew—the Nestlé Toll House recipe on the back of the yellow chocolate chip package. But when Kathleen made her first few batches, she didn't like how puffy and cakey they came out. So she started fiddling with the recipe. Kathleen added a little more butter in one batch and a little less flour in another. Some batches she cooked for longer, and for some batches she turned up the heat. Kathleen experimented in every way she could think of until they started to come out the way she preferred—thinner and crispier.

Kathleen visited the other farm stands in the area to taste her competition's product. She wanted her cookies to stand out from the other cookies in Southampton. As she gathered research, one thing jumped out at Kathleen: everyone else's cookies were small, about the size of a golf ball. "I wanted to do something that drew attention to my cookies, so I made them very large," Kathleen explains. "No one made large cookies back then."

Kathleen scooped huge mounds of cookie dough onto her baking tray and smiled. Approximately five inches in diameter, each cookie came out of the oven the size of a small plate. "And they were thin . . . with a little crisp chew," Kathleen shares. Using the advice of her father, Kathleen decided to price her cookies inexpensively so that no one could resist them. With each batch, she let them cool, then placed six huge cookies into a plastic bag and sealed it tight to lock in the freshness. Kathleen sold each bag for only 59 cents.

Kathleen's cookies were big, thin, chewy, and affordable. They were different from the cookies at anyone else's farm stand. And customers loved them!

Who Invented the Chocolate Chip Cookie?

Entrepreneur and chef Ruth Graves Wakefield invented the chocolate chip cookie in 1938. At the time, she owned and operated the Toll House Inn in Whitman, Massachusetts. One day, Ruth ran out of ingredients while she was baking cookies for her guests. Improvising, she chopped up a Nestlé chocolate bar, thinking it would melt. Instead, the chocolate chips kept their form and the chocolate chip cookie was born! Nestlé paid Ruth Wakefield a lifetime supply of chocolate in exchange for her secret Toll House recipe, which is always featured on the back of the yellow Nestlé chocolate chip package.

Word spread fast. Some customers drove to North Sea Farm for Tate's fresh eggs or vegetables and stumbled upon Kathleen's delicious dessert. Some customers drove to North Sea Farm stand just for Kathleen's cookies. Millie stepped in and helped Kathleen with the increased demand for her cookies. On her way home from work, Millie stopped at the local markets and picked up ingredients like flour, butter, and chocolate chips. Kathleen was grateful for her mother's help, but occasionally the products that Millie purchased disappointed Kathleen: "Sometimes she would buy ingredients on sale, and I refused to use them because they were not the quality I wanted!" Even though she was only 11, Kathleen had a keen sense of high quality and accepted nothing but the best in her baking.

Before long, Kathleen's cookies were the bestselling item at the farm stand. It was then that Tate realized his financial arrangement with Kathleen was not sustainable. Kathleen was selling so many cookies every single day, even more than he was selling eggs, fruit, or vegetables. Tate couldn't afford to pay for his daughter's ingredients and not receive any of the profits, so he renegotiated the deal with his daughter.

From then on, Kathleen would have to purchase her own ingredients, except for the fresh eggs from North Sea Farm, which Tate would continue to provide for free. Kathleen would keep all the profits from her cookie sales, which she could save or spend as she desired.

Since Kathleen's costs had gone up, she had to figure out a way to make the same amount of profit as she had before. She didn't want to increase the price of her cookies because her customers had gotten used to paying 59 cents a bag. She thought if she increased the price, she might lose some customers. So, Kathleen had another idea. She decided that instead of putting six cookies in a bag, she would put *five*. This simple change in her pricing strategy helped make up the difference in the extra costs of the ingredients. And her customers didn't seem to mind!

For nine straight summers, Kathleen worked extremely hard. She woke up with the sun and started her first batch of cookies. She baked and sold cookies all day until the sun went down in the evening and the farm stand closed. Kathleen's summers turned into 10-hour workdays, seven days a week. In addition to running her cookie business, Kathleen continued her other family responsibilities, which included tending the farm stand, collecting eggs from the chickens, and picking vegetables from the fields.

From 1969 to 1976, Kathleen's Cookies became known as the best cookies in Southampton, New York—a summer destination for the rich and famous. Her early customers included celebrities, business executives, models, and professional athletes. She met people from other countries, cultures, and backgrounds.

In 1977 Kathleen turned 18 and graduated from Southampton High School. That summer she made over $5,000 in cookie sales, enough to buy herself a used car and put herself through college.

Kathleen attended SUNY Cobleskill, a two-year college where she studied restaurant management and worked in a bakery on the weekends to earn extra money. After Kathleen graduated from college in 1979, she returned home to North Sea Farm to continue selling Kathleen's Cookies at the farm stand. But once she returned home, Kathleen learned that her mother had a different plan in mind.

Millie explained that Kathleen could no longer bake and sell cookies from North Sea Farm. It was time for her to open a bakery business. Kathleen didn't know anything about running her own business but trusted she could figure it out.

The next day, Kathleen headed into town to tour a vacant bakery. The air still smelled like flour. The space came with professional baking equipment and a large refrigerator. It had a quaint storefront to display her baked goods and a cash register already in place. The rent was $350 a month. Kathleen quickly did the math in her head and announced, "I'll take it."

It took four months to get Kathleen's Bake Shop ready to open. Kathleen used money-saving business tactics, like making her own labels from hand and using old farm equipment for the bakery's decor. She experimented with new recipes and perfected a full menu of pies, brownies, and cookies. But no matter how many new items she offered, her bestselling product from day one was Kathleen's Chocolate Chip Cookie.

Growing It

Kathleen's Bake Shop opened in 1980, and the *New York Times* declared it a must-see for visitors heading to the Hamptons. Customers flocked there. Kathleen worked 18-hour shifts to keep up with demand. She woke up hours before the sun rose, baked all morning, ran the bake shop all day, then cleaned in the evening. She was exhausted, but the work ethic she had learned from growing up on the farm carried her through the longest, most challenging days. When times were hardest, Tate reminded Kathleen how special she was, saying, "If everyone were like you, Kathleen, *their* name would be outside."

As the summer days wound down, so did business. By the time school was back in session and the cool fall air kept people from visiting the Hamptons, Kathleen's business had virtually vanished. She needed to figure out a way to keep business going during the winter, so she went to where her customers were: New York City.

Kathleen loaded up bags of cookies and walked into every specialty and gourmet shop in Manhattan. She introduced herself and offered free samples. Sometimes, the shop owners laughed in her face or rudely stated that *their mom* made better cookies than Kathleen. But most of the time, people fell in love with Kathleen's cookies and purchased big orders on the spot. Just like that, Kathleen had kept her business alive during the winter by creating a wholesale business—one that sells directly to other businesses instead of people.

As Kathleen's wholesale business grew in the winter and her bake shop sales exploded in the summer, space began to feel tight. It was time to expand, and Kathleen found the perfect spot—a building in town that had a better location and much more space. But to purchase the building, Kathleen needed $50,000 as a down payment. She only had $40,000 in savings. Her parents didn't have any money to spare, and she was unable to get a loan from the bank. Kathleen couldn't get ahold of that last $10,000. Her dreams started slipping through her fingers until one day, when the phone rang.

It was her father, Tate. What he had to share seemed nothing short of a miracle. An older woman in town had recently passed away and left Tate exactly $10,000 as a thank-you for helping her raise her chickens. Tate wanted to lend the entire amount to Kathleen so she could get her bigger bakery.

For 16 years—from 1983 to 1999—Kathleen's Bake Shop grew from a small store into an iconic location with cookie shipments around the nation. New cookie competitors like Mrs. Fields and Famous Amos popped up, but none offered a crisp, thin chocolate chip cookie like Kathleen. Business was booming!

But as Kathleen neared the age of 40, she was physically and mentally exhausted from years of long hours, and she hoped to cut back on her intense workdays and responsibilities. Two men approached her with a deal: they would become partners with Kathleen, manage the day-to-day business, and take over operations. In exchange, they each wanted one-third of the business.

Kathleen thought the agreement sounded fair. She longed for more time to travel with friends and relax with family, and she did want to take a step back from the day-to-day operations. However, Kathleen was making a huge mistake. By giving each of these new partners one-third of her business, she no longer was the majority owner of Kathleen's Bake Shop. In fact, these two new partners combined now owned two-thirds of the business and could make all the business decisions without Kathleen's consent. And unfortunately, that is exactly what they did.

The two new partners did *not* have Kathleen's best interests at heart. They let the quality of the products collapse. They ran up the company's debt and did not pay vendors. They even decided they wanted Kathleen removed from the company! Needless to say, Kathleen was furious. She had been bamboozled out of her own company. Kathleen took them to court, but after a long year of fighting to get Kathleen's Bake Shop back, Kathleen walked away with nothing.

The New Idea

Kathleen was 40 years old and had just lived through months of terrible lawsuits and lost the business she had built from scratch. But she never considered giving up. With fierce determination, Kathleen picked up the pieces of her life and her cookie business and started over.

Using the lessons learned from the previous two decades, Kathleen decided to launch a new company with a *better* cookie and a fresh brand. She pondered names for her new company, because she had even lost the right to use her own name! She wanted the new cookie business to have a name that sounded wholesome, heartfelt, approachable, and hardworking. And one name meant all those things to her: Tate, the name of her beloved father. Just like that, Tate's Bake Shop was launched.

Kathleen refocused her efforts on Tate's Bake Shop. She put everything into making Tate's Cookies the best cookie in the world. "I had the gift of dying and coming back," she explains, "learning what didn't work in that lifetime, and what will work in this lifetime."

Tate's Bake Shop launched in 2001. By 2011 *Consumer Reports* called Tate's Cookies the Best Cookie in America. Celebrities like chef and TV host Rachael Ray and movie star Gwyneth Paltrow sang Tate's Cookies' praises. Rachael Ray admitted that her own husband preferred Tate's Cookies over hers.

Southampton's prestigious and influential visitors and residents become one of Tate's Bake Shop's most powerful assets, supporting Kathleen's new business and driving sales to record levels. Kathleen released cookbooks and appeared on cooking shows, morning shows, and in magazine and newspaper articles. Before long, Tate's Bake Shop was bigger and better than Kathleen's Bake

Shop had ever been. "The biggest disaster of my life became the greatest gift of my life," Kathleen says.

In 2020 the *Washington Post* ranked 14 chocolate chip cookies available in grocery stores. Here's how they ranked:

1. Tate's Bake Shop
2. Pepperidge Farm Thin and Crispy
3. Chips Ahoy! Original
4. Trader Joe's
5. Enjoy Life
6. Chips Ahoy! Chunky
7. Famous Amos
8. Back to Nature Chocolate Chunk
9. 365 Organic
10. Lucy's Gluten-Free
11. Keebler Chips Deluxe
12. Grandma's
13. Entenmann's
14. Mrs. Fields

Kathleen King and Tate's Bake Shop Today

In 2014 Kathleen had reached her mid-50s and had a new goal—enjoy life more and give back to others. With no children of her own to take over the business, Kathleen made the decision to sell Tate's Bake Shop. Kathleen was approached by several companies who were interested in buying her company. Tate's Bake Shop eventually became part of Mondolēz International, a company that also owns Chips Ahoy!, Oreo, and Ritz. Today, Tate's Cookies are available all over the country and feature Kathleen's story on the back of every green package.

Kathleen King continues to live in Southampton and bakes every single day. She takes great pride in knowing that she showed the world that anyone with passion, determination, and a tremendous amount of hard work can build something incredible. Kathleen also enjoys sharing her story with kids, knowing well that "you never know who might change the world. All young people have the capacity." Kathleen King certainly did.

Follow Kathleen King and Tate's Bake Shop Online:

Website: www.tatesbakeshop.com

Instagram: @tatesbakeshop

Twitter: @TatesBakeShop

Facebook: Tate's Bake Shop

Stacy Madison: Stacy's Pita Chips

The line for Stacy Madison's sandwich cart in downtown Boston was a block long. Stacy knew that customers were willing to wait a short while to buy one of her famous pita-wrapped gourmet sandwiches, but a line a block long might cause them to go elsewhere. Thinking quickly, Stacy grabbed some of her pita chips and started passing out free samples to keep them engaged and waiting patiently.

"Wow!" she heard as they crunched on the chips. "These are incredible!" one customer exclaimed. "Are these for sale?" another customer asked.

"Yes, we sell them for one dollar a bag with your sandwich," Stacy replied, and thought to herself, *Maybe there's more to these pita chips than just a sidekick to her pita sandwiches.*

Stacy Madison grew up in a rural town in upstate New York. She lived in a small house with her parents, brother, and sister on Cherry Lane. Stacy's father was a psychologist, and her mother was a teacher. They believed kids, when not in school, should spend their free time playing and making their own fun. That also meant solving problems by themselves and learning how to get along with everyone. And that's exactly what Stacy did. She and the neighborhood kids rode bikes into town. They played at the park until sunset. They made campfires in the woods and sat around them sharing ghost stories. But Stacy's favorite game was when she and the neighborhood kids lined up their wagons on Cherry Lane. They tied them together with rope and hitched the front of the line of wagons to one of the boy's lawn mower tractor. The boy climbed onto his tractor, called out "All aboard the Cherry Lane train!" and off Stacy and her friends rode down Cherry Lane.

When Stacy wasn't at school or playing in the neighborhood, she often thought about grocery stores and the food that lined the shelves. She loved going to the grocery store with her mother and watched in wonder as customers lined up at the cashier's station with their baskets full of food. The cashiers quickly and seamlessly typed in the price of each item—there were no food scanners back then—and hit the ENTER button. The cashier's drawer popped open with a loud *ca-ching!* As soon as Stacy and her mom returned home with their bags of groceries, she unloaded each item and reenacted checking out her mom's groceries, but this time on the kitchen counter.

When Stacy entered junior high school, things became more difficult. She was not a strong student and had a hard time managing friendships. Some of the girls caused great stress in Stacy's life. One day, they acted like her best friends, but the next day Stacy would be the subject of their nasty bullying. The bullying became so bad that they threatened to hurt her and beat her up after school. Petrified, Stacy would often hide under a desk in a vacant classroom until everyone left, then walk home alone in the dark.

When Stacy turned 13, her family moved to Sharon, Massachusetts. She entered high school without any friends and continued to feel left out of social circles. Fortunately, Stacy and her brother had each other, and, over time, they helped one another meet some of the nicer kids in town. By the time Stacy turned 15, she had made a few close friends and was just starting her sophomore year.

Things were finally beginning to feel more settled until one day, while walking into town with a group of friends, Stacy was struck by a car. Family members rushed her to the hospital, where the doctor explained that she had suffered multiple broken bones in her arms and legs. For the next year, Stacy's life was put on hold as she healed in a full-body cast and relied on a wheelchair. As she was lying in bed day after day, her father often proudly stated how strong Stacy was. But Stacy didn't feel strong. She felt sad, lonely, and afraid. Life was not easy.

Twelve months later, Stacy's body eventually healed. After high school, she attended college at the University of Massachusetts at Amherst. On nights and weekends, she waitressed at a restaurant to help earn extra money. Stacy loved the way that working with food brought people together in a fun, social atmosphere. But despite her natural love for food, she didn't consider a career in it because her father had always suggested she take a safer, more predictable career path in social work.

Social workers help people who struggle with problems—anything from mental health problems to troubles at school or with family. Following in her father's footsteps, Stacy earned a master's degree in social work from California State University and took a job in Washington, DC, counseling pregnant women who were homeless or troubled in other ways. It paid $22,000 a year, which was not enough money to pay for her basic needs of rent, utilities, and food.

Struggling financially, Stacy wanted to find a better-paying job. She moved to Massachusetts and worked at a private practice that counseled married couples. And while the pay was better, Stacy realized that social work was not for her. It was not her passion. Stacy longed for something more exciting, something more social, something more hands-on. But what was it?

Stacy's First Jobs

By now, Stacy had become good friends with a man named Mark Andrus. He had a degree in psychology and was working at a hospital in Hawaii. In 1995 Stacy took a huge leap of faith. She quit her job in social work and jumped on a plane to join Mark in Hawaii.

Despite not having much money, Stacy and Mark made do with what they did have. They moved into a small apartment with only a bedroom and bathroom—that was it! They discovered how

to cook food without a kitchen and enjoyed making new recipes with different local ingredients. They bought an electronic wok and purchased fresh fish, vegetables, and fruit each day. Together, they chopped, seasoned, and cooked in their wok, then washed their dishes in the bathtub.

To help pay the bills, Stacy took a job as a manager at a restaurant. It was a popular spot, and the owners decided to open a second location. They hired Stacy to manage the second restaurant opening, and promised her a big bonus if it was a success. Stacy worked tirelessly, often for 12 or more hours a day, every day, without a day off. She did everything she could to ensure that the second restaurant opening was successful. And it was! In fact, during the restaurant's opening week, money came in so quickly that Stacy had to stuff bundles of cash into boxes and hide them in the restaurant's basement.

Confident with her job at successfully launching this second restaurant, she approached the owners and asked for her well-deserved bonus. But instead of giving it to her, they told her, "You're fired!"

"This was the best thing that ever happened to me," Stacy would later recall. "Right then and there I thought to myself, *If I can work this hard for someone else, why can't I do it for myself?*" Stacy finally knew what she wanted to do: she would become an entrepreneur.

Mark had also realized that the medical world was not right for him. The two friends thought about what excited them and what they were good at. An answer immediately popped into their heads—Stacy and Mark loved food and enjoyed cooking. They would create a food company together.

For three months, Stacy and Mark ran a small catering company out of their tiny apartment, before it was shut down by health inspectors who discovered the electric wok and bathtub dishwasher. If they were to proceed, Stacy and Mark would have to move into a commercial kitchen, which they didn't have the funds to do. So the two friends packed up their bags in 1996 and headed back home to Massachusetts.

It was 1997, and Stacy and Mark still dreamed of cooking delicious, healthy food for people. Their new vision was to open a sandwich cart in downtown Boston. But it wouldn't be just *any* sandwich cart. They would create and sell healthy and delicious gourmet sandwiches wrapped in fresh pita bread and topped with beautifully sliced tomatoes, crisp green lettuce, gourmet cheeses, and organic sprouts.

Stacy and Mark pooled their money and purchased a hot dog cart for $5,000. They redesigned it with a bright-green awning and attached an eye-catching sign that read STACY'S D'LITES. Each morning, Stacy and Mark filled the cart with fresh ingredients and loaded the bottom refrigeration section with ice to keep everything cool. They pushed their cart to the corner of Chauncy and Summer, in the heart of Boston's financial district. Day after day, Stacy and Mark prepared a delicious display of original, healthy pita sandwiches rolled tightly in paper. Almost immediately, Stacy's D'Lites was a tremendous hit! Hungry workers filed out of their office buildings at lunch hour and eagerly gobbled up the healthy, fresh lunch option.

Stacy and Mark quickly learned several important things about running a sandwich cart:

Rule #1: Only use the freshest ingredients. Pita bread didn't taste or roll well on the second day. That meant they needed to purchase fresh pita bread from a local bakery every morning.

Rule #2: Never run out of pita bread. If Stacy's D'Lites ran out of pita bread, they ran out of sandwiches. Customers didn't mind if they ran out of tomatoes or lettuce or sprouts, but no pita bread meant no sales. To avoid disaster, Stacy always bought too much pita bread each day. That also meant she had lots of leftover pita bread at the end of the day.

Rule #3: Keep your customers happy, especially if they must wait in a long line for your sandwiches.

By the time summer rolled around, the line to Stacy's D'Lites was long—very long. Her sandwiches were so popular that she feared customers wouldn't have the patience to wait their turn and would go eat elsewhere.

But Stacy was street-smart. At the end of each day, Stacy and Mark took the leftover pita bread, cut it up into wedges, seasoned the wedges with either garlic and parmesan or cinnamon and sugar, baked them in an eight-rack oven, then placed them into plastic bags and tied each bag with a ribbon. Stacy sold the bags for a dollar each, but when the line to her sandwich cart grew long, she walked up and down the block passing out free samples of her pita chips. And customers loved them! "We were basically making toast," Stacy later recalled. "Really, really good toast." By repurposing her unused inventory, Stacy had invented the pita chip.

Stacy's D'Lites continued to feed happy, hungry customers until the cold New England winter set in. Before long, the weather was unbearable. Stacy and Mark couldn't stand outside in the snow, sleet, and wind for hours anymore. Customers felt the same way, and found indoor options for their lunch break.

Stacy and Mark searched for an indoor spot to rent, perhaps in a food court or other popular lunch spot. But when the realtor told them they would be wedged between fast-food chains like Starbucks, Dunkin' Donuts, and Au Bon Pain, they feared an indoor spot would only be a waste of time and money. Sometimes, the realtor laughed at their small sandwich business, calling them a "dime a dozen." Stacy tried to find other indoor locations to park their sandwich cart, including Macy's, the big department store, but over and over again all she heard was "No!" Doors continued to slam in her face.

The Idea

Stacy and Mark had to make a decision: should they continue to try to find an indoor space for Stacy's D'Lites, or was there something to this pita chip idea? Customers adored the chips, but nothing like them existed. They didn't know if that was a good problem or a bad one. Could they grow a business around a new food? They considered how scalable the sandwich cart was versus the pita chip business. Scalability meant how big, fast, and easily they could grow the business.

Ultimately, Stacy and Mark decided their pita chip business could grow bigger and faster more quickly, and therefore was more scalable than their sandwich cart business. The decision was made—Stacy and Mark would close the sandwich cart and launch a pita chip company. They would call it Stacy's Pita Chips.

Stacy worked on packaging for their pita chips. She asked herself: What should it look like? What would it be made of? How big should the bag be? Should they offer different sizes or just one? She ultimately decided on one size with a plastic see-through window. She figured since no one knew what a pita chip was, it was important to show it through the packaging.

Stacy also started thinking about the shelf life of her product. At her food cart, customers ate the pita chips the day after they were baked, so she never worried about freshness, but a packaged product meant that the pita chips could sit on a shelf for days, weeks, or even months. Stacy tested the pita chips' shelf life and fiddled with the recipe until they came out just right and stayed fresher for longer.

Stacy took a few bags of her pita chips and walked into a small grocery store chain called Bread & Circus. They sold healthy, natural, and organic food. Stacy figured Bread & Circus was a good fit and asked to speak to the manager, explaining that she had created an all-natural pita chip snack. She gave him some samples. The manager took one bite, thought for a moment, and declared, "I love them. I'll put in an order." Just like that, Stacy had her first customer.

Stacy and Mark ordered $10,000 of bags and started preparing and packaging their pita chips. They worked day and night, slicing tens of thousands of pieces of pita bread and eventually developing biceps the size of softballs. They rented space from a local pretzel factory that had bigger baking racks. And when they weren't making pita chips, Stacy and Mark brought samples to grocery stores and sandwich shops. Orders continued to come in from small gourmet delis and health-focused grocery stores. Stacy quickly learned that the most important marketing they could do was to provide free samples of the product. In fact, *Sample, Sample, Sample* became her mantra.

But then one day, a huge problem struck: the window of the bag was failing them. The plastic see-through screen was flimsy, and when combined with the pointy edges of the pita chips, disaster struck. The pita chips pierced the plastic window, and most of the chips spilled during shipping. Customers grew frustrated, and a huge amount of product was wasted. Stacy and Mark ended up throwing out thousands of dollars' worth of bags and scrambling to find a replacement—something more durable for their sharp snacks.

The two founders continued to face new challenges week after week. They realized they needed to learn more about their industry and how to streamline the pita chip–making process. Their biceps couldn't keep up with the demand!

One day, Stacy and Mark went on a factory tour of Cape Cod Potato Chips. The tour guide led the group to the assembly line where the potatoes were cleaned, sliced, fried, salted, and bagged. Stacy's eyes lit up. This is what Stacy's Pita Chip needed—a factory like this! Stacy asked hundreds of questions that day. Who made that machine? How did the machine slice the potatoes? What happened if one potato was small and one was large? How did the slicer work? How long did the machine last? How many chips were produced in a day, a week, a month? How much did the machine cost? How did the machine put the right amount of chips in a bag? How did it seal the bags?

After their factory tour, it was clear that Stacy and Mark needed a pita chip machine—one that would take fresh pita bread and slice it just right. But a machine like that did not exist because no one had ever made a pita chip before. Every slicing machines they researched took raw fruits and vegetables and sliced them in a circle. But Stacy didn't want circle chips: she wanted square pita chips.

Then, one day, Stacy and Mark came across something extraordinary. It was a carrot-cutting machine that the Campbell Soup Company had used to cut up carrots into square shapes back in 1964. A friend of theirs understood machinery. He thought he could reconfigure the square cutting blades so that it didn't cut in a small soup-carrot shape but rather a medium-size pita chip shape.

Stacy and Mark trusted their friend. They purchased the machine, and their friend spent a day taking the machine apart and putting it back together. Stacy's head spun and her heart raced as she feared the worse—that the machine might not work. At the end of the day, the friend announced it was ready. The three of them took a deep breath together to calm their nerves.

"Are you ready?" the friend asked. Stacy and Mark nodded anxiously. "OK, here we go!" He dropped in a few loaves of pita bread at the mouth of the machine. The machine grumbled. It whirled. It made some other funny noises . . . and a few moments later . . . perfectly cut pita chips came out the other side. The three friends cheered with delight: "Holy cow! It's a pita chip!"

Buying machines, bread, ingredients, bags all cost money. Lots of money. To fund the business Stacy and Mark did everything they could to make ends meet. They loaned money from the bank. They also ran up their credit cards. They borrowed from friends and family members who believed in their idea. They lived in small apartments and drove beat-up old cars to help save money. But they held on to one very special thing—their equity (or ownership) in the business. Stacy and Mark each owned 50 percent of Stacy's Pita Chips.

Florence Parpart, Inventor of the Refrigerator

Florence Parpart was born in Hoboken, New Jersey, and grew up to be one of the most successful inventors and female entrepreneurs of the early 20th century. In 1900 Florence invented an improved street-cleaning machine that she sold throughout the country. In 1914

Florence invented what is now known as the modern electric refrigerator. With her invention, people could keep food stored longer and in better condition. Florence created a successful marketing campaign around her refrigerator and sold it at trade shows around the country.

Growing It

By 2001, Stacy's Pita Chips was growing at a rapid rate. The product was in national grocery stores like Trader Joe's and Whole Foods as well as in club stores like Costco and Sam's Club. Customers all over the country were falling in love with the crispy, healthier chip that paired perfectly with hummus, cheese, or on its own.

Stacy Pita Chips employed 300 people, and just as they put their heart into making a great product, Stacy and Mark put their heart into making Stacy's Pita Chips a great place to work. They enforced a hiring policy called Click and Tick, which meant that a person must "click" with the other employees before they were hired. Stacy also wanted to understand what made each of her employees "tick," or made them happy. For example, one employee liked to leave work in time to coach his kids' sports team while another employee enjoyed teaching a yoga class once a week. Stacy and Mark believed that if they respected what was important to their employees, their employees would respect what was important to them—Stacy's Pita Chips.

As Stacy's Pita Chips hit new levels of growth, Stacy started to realize that she was ready both financially and mentally to start a family. And while she and Mark had been married for a short time, they were now divorced, so Stacy decided to have a family on her own. In 2003 Stacy gave birth to healthy twin girls, Morgan and Samantha, who became the light of her life. Soon, Morgan, Samantha, and Stacy's 110-pound dog became regular visitors to the office.

As the days ticked away, juggling being a single mom and managing a multimillion-dollar company was taking a toll on Stacy. She felt guilty for not spending as much time with her children as she would have liked, and she wasn't as happy as she used to be managing the business. She felt that the business was running her, instead of her running the business.

Mark was also thinking about things other than pita chips. He longed to travel the world, but felt he couldn't do that as long as he owned 50 percent of Stacy's Pita Chips.

And then the phone started to ring. Several of the biggest food companies were interested in buying Stacy's Pita Chips. Stacy and Mark decided together it was the right time to sell their business. "We built our business because we wanted to do something that we loved to do every day and make a living doing it," Stacy explained. "And that was it—there's was no exit strategy." But now they were being handed an end to their entrepreneurial journey.

In 2006 Stacy and Mark sold Stacy's Pita Chips to PepsiCo for $250 million. PepsiCo owned snack brands like Frito-Lay, and the two founders felt like it was the best fit for their brand. But selling a business was a bit like handing over your first child. Something Stacy had built from nothing was suddenly no longer hers, and it made her feel lost. In fact, she felt a wild mix of emotions, including excitement, fear, frustration, gratitude, confusion, and loneliness.

Stacy Madison and Stacy's Pita Chips Today

Stacy moved her family to a nice house in a suburb of Boston where her kids could ride bikes and play in the park, just as she did as a child. But she just couldn't shake the entrepreneur in her. In 2019 Stacy hired some of her former Stacy's Pita Chip employees and created a new company called BeBold Bars. Today, BeBold Bars makes all-natural protein bars for healthy, active people. Stacy also volunteers for the foundation Stacy's Rise Project, which helps female entrepreneurs start their businesses.

Thinking back on her entrepreneurial journey, Stacy fondly remembers the excitement of the first time she saw a woman put a package of Stacy's Pita Chips into her shopping cart at a grocery store. Stacy raced over to the woman and excitedly announced, "Hi! I'm Stacy and those are my chips!" The woman furrowed her eyebrows at Stacy and promptly stated, "No, they're not. They're mine!" Then she quickly pushed her cart off to the checkout line.

Follow Stacy Madison and Stacy's Pita Chips Online:

Websites: www.stacyssnacks.com, www.stacyssnacks.com/riseproject, and www.beboldbars.com

Instagram: @_stacymadison, @stacys, and @beboldbars

Twitter: @StacysPitaChips and @beboldbars

Facebook: Stacy's Pita Chips and BeBOLD Bars

Christina Tosi: Milk Bar

It was Sunday morning, and, as usual, Christina had arrived early to work at the restaurant where she was a pastry chef. Christina enjoyed baking desserts for the staff each day, which they enjoyed at "Family Meal" before the customers came in to dine. This particular morning, Christina had pie on her mind. She pulled out the basic ingredients: flour, sugar, eggs, and butter, then wondered what kind of pie she should create. But when she opened the fridge, she couldn't locate any spare ingredients. And because it was Sunday, there wouldn't be any deliveries that day.

Christina racked her brain for a recipe that would just use the basics, and vaguely remembered a recipe for something called Chess Pie. It originated in the Deep South and was a pie that people baked when they didn't have the star ingredients on hand, like apples, blueberries, or pumpkin. Originally called Just Pie, the name morphed into Chess Pie as those with a deep Southern twang passed the recipe on from one person to another.

Christina whisked together the basic ingredients she had and threw it into the oven. When the timer when off, she pulled it out to find a thin, flat, light-brown pie. It looked awful! Embarrassed, she delivered it to Family Meal and left the room. Moments later, something caught her ear. Her fellow workers were going bonkers! Christina stepped into the other room and was bombarded with comments and questions: "What is this pie?" "What's in it?" "How did you make it?" "This is amazing!"

Christina's new pie soon became a bestseller and was eventually named Milk Bar Pie.

Christina Tosi was born in 1981 and grew up outside Washington, DC. Her father's family had immigrated from Northern Italy, and Christina was constantly surrounded by strong role models, Italian women who proved they could do it all.

As a young girl, Christina worked hard at school, studied feverishly, and received excellent grades. She played sports outside school, and she usually "followed the rules," never wanting to let her parents down. "Tosis don't get anything but A's," Christina recalled her father telling her year after year. The expectation was that children in the Tosi family worked hard in school, got a well-respected job, and loved what they did. And while Christina was raised in a strict household that constantly pushed her to be the best she could be, there was one place in her life where the rules could be broken: in the kitchen.

From as early as she can remember, Christina's fondest memories are baking in the kitchen. Baking was fun. Baking was filled with family. And baking just tasted so good! Christina was a bright, curious kid and discovered that when she baked in the kitchen, she could safely experiment with different recipes, fun ingredients and new techniques, and that was always OK and allowed. She could even "act out" a bit by stealing extra cookie dough when the grown-ups weren't looking, or by licking the icing off the spatula.

Christina started bringing her masterpieces to school the day after she baked them. Friends, teachers, and classmates were amazed by the taste and variety of Christina's baked goods. And she loved the attention. Before long, Christina showed up almost every day of school with a new, freshly baked dessert. Even as a young girl, Christina's heart sung to see how her baking brought people together and created happiness.

But as Christina grew older, she was constantly reminded that Tosis work hard in school and get well-respected jobs. So, she attended the University of Virginia and majored in applied mathematics and Italian. However, unlike baking, these subjects did not make her heart sing. In fact, Christina left college after a year, transferred to James Madison University, and decided to study abroad in Italy. There she soaked up the culture, perfected the language, and again excelled in academics.

Christina graduated from college in only three years. (It takes most people four years to complete college.) As soon as she graduated, reality soaked in. Christina asked herself, "What is it that you're passionate about?"

Rosenella Winifred Cruciani Totino, Inventor of the Frozen Pizza

Rose, like Christina, was the daughter of Italian immigrants. She enjoyed making pizza for friends and opened up a pizza parlor in Minneapolis, Minnesota, in 1951. The shop was a huge success, and it made Rose contemplate other ways her customers could enjoy pizza. In 1962 Rose created a separate business that invented and sold the first frozen pizzas. In 1975 Pillsbury bought Rose's business for $20 million and made her the company's first female vice president.

Christina's First Jobs

One thing immediately popped into her head—baking! Christina loved to bake. She baked every day and everywhere. She baked to de-stress or to make friends. She baked for herself, for family, and for strangers. Christina just wanted to bake all the time! And it dawned on her that there was only one place to go to find her dream job: New York City.

Christina enrolled in culinary school as a pastry chef. There, she learned baking techniques and made connections with other like-minded chefs. But Christina felt like she was late to the game compared with the other pastry chefs who had known what they wanted to do with their lives for years. In order to catch up, Christina decided she needed to land a job in the best restaurant in town. She convinced the manager at one of New York City's top restaurants, a place called Bouley, to hire her.

It was grueling! Christina worked six days a week, every week. And the days were incredibly long. Five of the days, she worked from 11:00 AM to 3:00 AM, and on the sixth day, she worked from 7:00 AM to 3:00 AM. On those days, she only had four hours to sleep, eat, and shower.

But Christina was stubborn and tough and recalled, "Somehow, I was totally built for the ride of it." After two years of working at Bouley, Christina longed to learn something new in the world of restaurants and desserts. It was time to move on, and she found a job at another hot New York City restaurant called wd~50.

There Christina not only shined as a pastry chef but also helped the owner and head chef with other aspects of the business, including figuring out the legal paperwork that the health department needed. Christina's studious mind came in handy as she managed a 60-page analysis that explained in detail how wd~50 handled complicated cooking methods.

Word spread of Christina's bright mind and unique talent for managing tough jobs. Soon, other top chefs in New York City wanted help with similar health department legal issues. This all led to Christina meeting one of the city's most famous chefs, David

Chang. David Chang ran the world-famous Momofuku restaurant. In 2005 David asked Christina to come work for him. She realized this was a big opportunity in her career, especially since David had never employed a pastry chef before, nor even sold dessert! Christina agreed, becoming the first female chef on his team, and was given the freedom to continue to invent wacky and wild deserts. Her Milk Bar Pie had become a hit, and every day she experimented with how to add fun flavors to everyday desserts: "I was thinking through basic desserts like pancetta . . . and thought, 'Wouldn't it be cool if it was flavored [with] something different?'"

Eventually, Christina's mathematical mind determined that milk was the common denominator in most desserts. Almost every single dessert had some form of milk in it, and if she could flavor the milk, she could flavor the entire dessert. So, Christina started to ponder, *What could I flavor milk with?* Day after day, Christina walked up and down the aisles of the grocery store, looking at products and asking herself, *Could you be a flavor of milk?* Finally, she hit the cereal aisle. A light bulb went off: cereal milk!

Christina infused milk with cereal flavors and started making milk-based desserts like ice cream and panna cotta with cereal milk. New Yorkers loved them!

The Idea

By 2008 Christina knew who she was as a baker. She was not a pastry chef in a fine dining restaurant. Instead, she was all about homemade, creative, wacky, accessible, and sharable desserts. And David Chang recognized that Christina was on to something groundbreaking.

He suggested that Christina convert an old laundromat next to his restaurant into a bakery. He lent her the money and said, "Go figure out how to sign the lease and let's go. When is it going to open?" Christina, like always, knew she just had to just jump in and figure it out, rather than get scared and back away. So, away she went.

At 27 years old with no plan at all, Christina launched Milk Bar.

Growing It

Milk Bar was quirky from day one. It projected a bright pink MILK neon sign and offered cookies, brownies, and pies that have never been created before. Flavors like Cornflake Marshmallow Chocolate Chip Cookie and Compost Cookie, with potato chips, pretzels, and coffee, filled the shelves. Cakes had no frosting on their sides so customers could see each layer of cake and filling. People were wowed, and a line of customers filled her store all day long.

The staff of four worked tirelessly day and night to make Milk Bar a success. But it was hard work. Christina did not sleep much, and never went out. She didn't spend any money, and everything she made went back into Milk Bar.

In 2009 Christina had her first big break. A prominent CNN host named Anderson Cooper was guest-hosting a daytime talk show called *Regis & Kelly*. He announced on air that he was wild for Milk Bar's pie, and just like that Christina's phone didn't stop ringing. As she listened to messages from eager customers across the nation, she kept hearing the same thing over and over. People outside New York City wanted to enjoy her crazy baked goods, too! At that moment, Christina recognized that this was yet another career-changing moment, explaining, "When opportunity knocks, what are you going to say? You rise!"

Christina started an online business that shipped her innovative desserts beyond the Big Apple. She also opened new locations. By 2012, Milk Bar had nine Milk Bar bakeries in cities across North America, including Toronto, Canada; Las Vegas, Nevada; and Washington, DC. The buzz around the wacky pastry chef just got bigger.

In 2015 Christina joined the cast of *MasterChef* and *MasterChef Junior* on Fox television as a judge alongside the world-renowned chef Gordon Ramsay. It was then that world learned what a star Christina was.

Ina Garten, Entrepreneur of Barefoot Contessa

Ina Garten was working at the White House on the budget for enriched uranium program when she became bored and realized, *Life has to be more fun than this.* Ina's husband encouraged her to open a catering business in town, insisting she was a very good cook. Ina made an offer on a location. The owners called her back to say, "Thank you very much, I accept your offer." Ina immediately freaked out! But after a few years of running her catering business, Ina wanted to write a cookbook. Her first cookbook, *The Barefoot Contessa*, was an instant hit, and many cookbooks followed. Television shows came next. Ina Garten is one of today's most successful food entrepreneurs with a net worth of more than $40 million.

Christina Tosi and Milk Bar Today

Christina has continued to expand Milk Bar into new cities and is always launching new recipes as well as offering her wacky favorites. She remains stubborn as the company grows, insisting that it maintain the same values and work ethic that made Milk Bar a success from the start. Her online business continues to thrive and makes up a third of her total sales.

But despite the spotlight and success, Christina vows that at the end of the day not much has changed in her life. She still loves to bake every day, noting that it's really nice to do something with "our hands, not our thumbs."

Follow Christina Tosi and Milk Bar Online:

Website: https://milkbarstore.com/

Instagram: @christinatosi and @milkbarstore

Twitter: @christinatosi and @milkbarstore

Facebook: Milk Bar

Part II: Health and Beauty

Lisa Price: Carol's Daughter

Lisa Price was a big Prince fan. She loved Prince's music, and one evening she found herself standing next to him at a club. Awestruck, she happened to notice something delightful about the famous pop star—he smelled like a garden of flowers. And when Prince walked away, the scent disappeared.

Lisa wondered if Prince always smelled that good. Turned out, he did! Prince traveled with a buffet of scented oils and wore various scents on different parts of his body. In his boots was one scent, on his clothes was another. Lisa couldn't help but wonder if her gift of identifying scents and her meeting Prince was a sign that bigger things were on the horizon.

Lisa Price was born on May 18, 1962, in Brooklyn, New York. Always a bright student, Lisa's parents, Carol and Robert, pushed her in school and expected straight As. Lisa attended El Hajj Malik El Shabazz Elementary School in Brooklyn. Her grandfather usually picked her up after school, and their walks home were Lisa's favorite:

"He always had colorful conversation for me and he always had a treat in his pocket for me. And, you know, we just had these great talks."

Lisa attended middle school at St. Augustine's in the Bronx where her teacher, Mrs. Jackman, became a mentor. Mrs. Jackman would separate the stronger students from the others and challenge them to their limits. It was then that Lisa was identified as one of the top students in her class.

Lisa took high-school-level classes when she was in seventh grade. She entered Fiorello H. LaGuardia High School of Music & Art and Performing Arts in New York City at the age of 12, and started to dream of becoming a singer and actress when she grew up. To get to the high school, however, was quite a journey. Each day was pretty much the same, Lisa rode the train for 90 minutes to school, and in the afternoon, another 90 minutes straight back. Once home, she ran upstairs and into her bedroom to do her homework and study. A homebody, Lisa enjoyed being inside rather than playing outside with other kids on the block.

For fun, Lisa liked to browse expensive stores looking at the latest fashions, then shop at less expensive stores and try to match them. She also had a keen sense of smell. Some of the girls in school wore perfumes called Bonne Bell, Love's Baby Soft, and one that smelled like green apples. But there was one particular girl in high school named Flame who wore scented oils. Lisa was mesmerized by Flame and the different aromas that wafted around her each day. One day, she smelled like strawberry, the next day like frankincense. These were scents that didn't come in perfumes.

By the time she was 15, Lisa had achieved such high grades that she was on track to graduate high school at the age of 16. And while her father tried to accelerate that pace even faster, Lisa pushed back. Instead, she dreamed of attending the University of Miami with her best friend, Dawnn Lewis, and together they planned to study music and drama. Dawnn went on to be an actress in Hollywood, but Lisa's life took a different path.

In 1978 Lisa graduated high school and ended up staying in New York City, attending City College of New York. But it became clear that this wasn't the place for her. Lisa learned that in a college with such a large campus and classroom sizes, she was no longer a star student. In fact, the opposite was true—she felt invisible. Lisa stopped going to her classes, and when no one noticed, she stopped turning in her assignments. Before long, Lisa, the star student, had flunked out of college and dropped out.

Lisa's First Jobs

Lisa's parents disapproved of her dropping out of college, but she had already made up her mind. It was time to leave home and start her life as an adult. Lisa took a job at American Express, moved in with a boyfriend, and discovered what it was like to live without the academic pressures that encompassed her childhood.

From 1978 to 1982, Lisa learned a lot about herself. She lived a very clean life that focused on eating and drinking only organic and vegan foods. She meditated and practiced yoga daily.

Over the next few years, Lisa held several jobs, including being a messenger for the United Nations and a singer in a girls' musical group called Tuxedo Gold.

One day, Lisa and her Tuxedo Gold friends were walking down the streets of New York City and passed a Muslim man who had a display of various scented oils for sale. Lisa smelled the oils and asked, "Would you mix them for me?" The man didn't understand what mixing oils meant and Lisa clarified, "Well, if I want like half of this, and half of this, will you mix it?" He answered, "Yeah, I'll mix it."

Lisa went home with her new oils, not realizing at the time that she had a special gift for mixing, blending, and layering scents. She wore her new oil blends to work, and people started to notice how wonderful they smelled. But when she returned to purchase more products from the man, he was nowhere to be found.

In 1988 a friend called her, excited that he had found a place in New York City where Lisa could buy and mix her own essential oils. She took a bus across town, spent $40, and came home with a bag of ingredients. That evening, she mixed and matched oils, writing down a recipe for a scent she called Number One, her first fragrance. It smelled crisp, clean, and fresh, almost like lettuce straight from the garden.

In 1990 Lisa took a job as an assistant to a writer for *The Cosby Show*. At the time, *The Cosby Show* was one of the biggest shows on television and featured a smart, funny, and wholesome African American family. America fell in love with *The Cosby Show*, and Lisa fell in love with her job, hoping to work there for the rest of her life. After work, Lisa found joy experimenting with and mixing scented oils, also blending them with unscented body creams and lotions to create wonderful body care products. She gifted them to friends and family and brought them into work for the actors to use.

During this time, Lisa purchased a book about essential oils that helped her understand the chemistry behind how oils blended with different products. But when she tried to make her own body butter, a thick type of lotion she named after her grandmother's butter cake, she struggled. Despite following the recipe, carefully writing down exactly what she did each time, and trying to tweak it, the lotions and body butters separated and became messy. And when they cooled in the fridge, they came out stiff and oily—not how she wanted.

One evening, while Lisa worked on her lotions, she glanced up at the television and saw a Duncan Hines commercial. The cake batter was being whipped up with a hand mixer, and, right before her eyes, it turned into a thick, creamy consistency. Lisa wondered if she could whip her body butter with a hand mixer while it cooled. It couldn't hurt to try, and just like that, it whipped into the perfect consistency under the power of a hand mixer. Jumping for joy, Lisa ran around the apartment yelling, "I figured out how to make the butter! I figured out how to make the butter!"

Sarah Breedlove / Madame C. J. Walker

When Sarah Breedlove was 20 years old, she moved to St. Louis with her two-year-old daughter and worked as a laundress, which left her skin and scalp dry, itchy, and full of dandruff. To help ease her discomfort, Sarah learned about different hair products and treatments at her brothers' barber shop and started to experiment, ultimately creating her own line of products.

In 1906 Sarah changed her name to Madame C. J. Walker (she had recently married a man named Charles Walker) and began a business that sold her beauty care products door-to-door. She also taught Black women how to care for their hair, how to become entrepreneurs, and how to be financially independent. Between 1911 and 1919, Madame C. J. Walker trained and employed thousands of women and became America's first female self-made millionaire as well as one of the richest African Americans in the United States.

The Idea

Lisa's mother, Carol, loved her daughter's body butter and thought it was good enough to sell. She suggested Lisa sell it at the local flea market at their church. Lisa wasn't so sure and asked, "What am I gonna put it in?" Her mother suggested baby-food jars, so Lisa pulled out several baby-food jars from the recycling bin. (Carol had just adopted a baby girl.) Lisa sterilized them and scooped the body butter into the jars, then drew labels on white file-folder labels and carefully placed them on each jar. Next, Lisa thought about a name for her product and made a list of who she was and what she stood for. When she read back the list, one name gave her goose bumps: Carol's Daughter.

On May 25, 1993, Lisa set up a table at the flea market and sold out of every jar of Carol's Daughter body butter. She made more and brought them to a different flea market the next weekend. She sold out again. But even though Lisa spent the summer making and selling her body butter at local markets and street fairs, she still considered it to be a hobby. Until one day Lisa turned on *The Oprah Winfrey Show*.

The hit talk show featured a group of female entrepreneurs, women who had started their companies with virtually no money. Lisa listened carefully as these women explained what it took to be successful. One entrepreneur said, "You must have repeat customers." Another entrepreneur said, "You must know who your demographic is." The next entrepreneur said, "You have to *really* be passionate about what you do because it takes so long for you to make money." This woman's test for true entrepreneurial passion was, "If someone woke you up in the middle of the night and said, *Go do this thing*, would you get up out of your bed and go do it?" Lisa's answer was YES! This was her aha moment. She was an entrepreneur.

Growing It

Over the following year, Lisa's life went something like this: she worked a nine-to-five job, Monday to Friday. During that time, people called asking for Carol's Daughter creams, shampoos, oils, and body butters. Lisa took careful notes on each call, then when Friday night came around, she made her products. Early Saturday morning, she displayed them beautifully in a room of her apartment, and by breakfast time, customers rang her doorbell, excited to shop in Lisa's apartment, stocking up on their favorite Carol's Daughter's products.

Lisa kept a careful database of each customer's address, held special holiday events, and send out postcards to her ever-growing list of customers. "Right before Christmas, you would get a postcard to let you know that the holiday sale event is taking place on December 12th, and December 19th, and, and my house would just get turned into a store," Lisa remembered. "And, initially, it was my family coming over and having tea and doing a little Christmas shopping . . . then after a while it was not family. It was strangers and my family stop[ped] coming 'cause it was so crowded with other people!"

In 1995 Saturday sales had grown so much that Lisa needed to quit her day job and focus on Carol's Daughter full time. By 1997 Lisa was married, had one child named Forest, and was pregnant with her second child (who would be named Ennis). They moved into a bigger house, and, just before she gave birth, *Essence* magazine interviewed her for an article they called "People to Know."

Lisa incorrectly assumed this article would feature several interesting people and thought little of it. But it turned out that *Essence* was running a huge article just about Lisa Price and her company, Carol's Daughter. The article hit the same week Ennis was born, and by the time she returned home from the hospital with her new baby, the Carol's Daughter voice mail was completely full with product requests, and the line never stopped ringing! "We had a schedule between taking care of a nineteen-month-old, feeding the new baby, we had to keep checking the voice mail because it was filling up. And the phone would just ring and ring and ring, all day long . . . I would like look at the clock and say, 'It's one o'clock, when was the last time you checked the messages?'" Her husband would answer, "At eleven." Then Lisa would panic, "Eleven, oh, God it's full again, get the phone, get the phone!'"

Lisa turned the first floor of their home into a showroom, and before long, she had already shipped tens of thousands of her beauty products to customers across the country. She knew it was time to move into a real storefront.

One night, Lisa had a dream. In it, a real estate broker was telling her to move into a store formerly used by Spike Lee. When she woke up, Lisa contacted her realtor. Doubtful she could afford the rent, she still thought the dream was a sign and asked to see the space. It was perfect. It had a storefront plus space for shipping catalog orders and making gift baskets. But the rent was expensive. She needed to come up with a $14,000 down payment to cover four months of rent. Lisa didn't have $14,000.

Lisa recounted, "My husband had some money in the bank that he had gotten from a court settlement and that was almost $5,000. We emptied out the kids' piggy banks, we emptied out our savings account.

We got out our credit cards to see what cash advances we could get. We went through pockets, and sofa cushions, and found whatever we could find." She made the $14,000 deposit deadline by a matter of minutes.

On August 21, 1999, the first official Carol's Daughter store opened. By 9:00 AM, a line had formed down the block—and it didn't stop the entire day. Dozens of people packed the store so tightly that there were times Lisa couldn't see to the opposite wall. It was a great first day.

From there, word of mouth grew exponentially. Carol's Daughter was one of the only companies that catered to African American hair and body needs. Lisa had filled a niche in the beauty care market.

Iman Mohamed Abdulmajid

Iman Abdulmajid is a Somali American model who faced moments of discrimination during her modeling career and was inspired to do something about it. During her first photo shoot, a makeup artist asked Iman if she brought her own foundation because he didn't have anything in her color. Over the years, Iman found this to be a regular occurrence at photo shoots—makeup artists asked women of color to bring their own foundation, but never the White models.

Iman was already making her own makeup to match her skin color, and in 1994 launched IMAN Cosmetics, the first cosmetics and skin care collection designed for all women with skin of color. Iman explained the mission

> behind her company at the time as "appealing to a deep psychological need that I think all Black women needed at that time: To be told that they were beautiful, invited to sit at the table, and courted in high style: women of all skin tones want to look good when they rule the world."

In 2002 *The Oprah Winfrey Show* called Lisa. The producers wanted her on the show to share her entrepreneurial story. Lisa was thrilled and appeared on the show on June 25, 2002. With Oprah's seal of approval, business took off. By 2005 celebrities like Will Smith, Jay-Z, and Jada Pinkett Smith sang Carol's Daughter's praises and became investors. With their help, sales grew to tens of millions of dollars, and her products could be found in stores like Sephora and Macy's.

By 2014 Carol's Daughter had become a global brand, and Lisa knew her company needed a more advanced infrastructure to take the wheel. She decided to sell Carol's Daughter to beauty conglomerate L'Oréal.

Lisa Price and Carol's Daughter Today

Lisa's mother passed away on Valentine's Day 2003, but Carol watched her daughter's success grow from a hobby to a thriving business that brought beauty and happiness to millions of people of color. Carol saw her daughter appear on *The Oprah Winfrey Show*, and, most important, Carol supported her talented daughter through thick and thin. Throughout the years, Carol was her daughter's rock, staying positive the entire time, and assuring Lisa that she could indeed do it all in business *and* be a great mom.

Looking back, Lisa remembers one particular day early in the business when holiday orders were through the roof and she wasn't sure how she was going to fulfill them all. She had to make the product, package it, and ship it out in time. Frazzled, she called her mother. Carol calmed her down, saying, "That's the easy part. What if you didn't have orders? That would be the harder part. . . . You have the orders! You have their credit card numbers! Money is sitting there waiting for you. . . . Go make yourself a cup of tea and we'll figure it out." Each time Lisa felt like she was in over her head, Carol would insist she make a cup of tea, and they would talk through the challenges, always figuring out a plan that kept the business moving forward.

Follow Lisa Price and Carol's Daughter Online:

Website: www.carolsdaughter.com

Instagram: @IamLisaPrice and @carolsdaughter

Twitter: @IAmLisaPrice and @carolsdaughter

Facebook: Carol's Daughter

Payal Kadakia: ClassPass

When Payal Kadakia was in third grade, she had already become quite good at Indian folk dance and longed to share her gift with her classmates. So when the school held a talent show, Payal signed up to perform. She draped herself with a beautiful Indian sari. She pulled back her long, smooth dark hair and she stepped onto the stage. As Payal began her dance to traditional Indian folk music, something terrible happened. A few of the kids started laughing. Then more kids started laughing. Some of them even booed! Payal's sister, Avani, who was in the audience, turned red with embarrassment. It was at that moment that Payal decided she would never again blend her two lives—her Indian life and American life—together. Or so she thought.

Payal Kadakia was born in 1982 to parents who believed nothing was more important than her education. They had even risked their lives for it, emigrating from India in the 1970s after a relative gave them two plane tickets to America as a wedding gift. It was a gift that meant a better life for their children.

The Kadakia family moved to Randolph, New Jersey, and bought a house in a suburb known for having one of the best education systems in the state. While Payal's parents could barely afford the house they purchased, they both held jobs as chemists and worked day and night to make ends meet. Payal's father worked during the day while Payal's mother stayed home and took care of the girls. In the evening, the roles reversed: Payal's mother went to work, and her father stayed home to be with the girls and helped with homework.

School and homework always came first in the Kadakia family. One afternoon, Payal noticed the dishwasher hadn't been unloaded and asked her mother if she could help with the kitchen chores. Her mother responded, "Only if your homework is finished." And while nothing was more important than education to Payal's parents, over time something became more important to Payal: dancing.

When Payal was quite young, she started to recognize that she was living what seemed to be two separate lives. From Monday to Friday, Payal attended school with her White friends and classmates. She worked very hard at school, kept quiet in social situations, and received excellent grades. But she often felt lonely. No one at school looked like her. No one in her town looked like her. In fact, no one on TV or in any of her books looked like her. "There were only five Indian families in my entire town and only one Indian student other than me in my class," Payal remembers. She was picked on and bullied for looking and being different. There were days she begged her mom not to go to school, even at a very young age.

On the weekends, however, Payal lived a completely different life. Her parents brought her and Avani to a nearby community where other Indian families celebrated together. They ate traditional Indian food and gathered for beautiful festivals that celebrated the Indian culture they loved. And it was there that Payal started to dance.

Payal was only three years old when her mother introduced her to a friend named Usha Patel. Usha taught Indian American girls and women traditional classical and folk Indian dance. Payal's mother thought that if Payal learned how to dance traditional dances, she would better appreciate her cultural identity.

At first Payal thought traditional folk dance was boring. Like many young American girls, she longed to dance to something more exciting and modern. She was also a little scared of Usha, who demanded hard work from her students, perfect grades in school, and promptness and respect at each lesson. But as Payal returned for dance class week after week, she started to appreciate the steps that moved together in unison. She learned how each dance was only as good as the weakest link in the group. She appreciated that hard work and practice made not only her performance better, but also made the group better. She loved the way each dance told a different story of Indian women from history, whether it was gathering water from the river or churning butter. Payal also began watching the older girls dance under Usha's instruction. They were stunning. With their graceful rhythms and their in-unison dance steps, the older girls looked like Indian goddesses in Payal's eyes. And since Payal didn't have anyone at her school to look up to, the older girls at Usha's dance class became her role models. Payal wanted to be just like them one day.

As Indian dance became more important in Payal's life, she began watching Hindi films, often called Bollywood films, where beautiful Indian women danced with expression and charisma. They were confident, they were alive, and they touched their audience in such moving ways. Payal knew this was who she wanted to be!

As Payal grew older and entered high school, she became very good at living a dual life. During the weekdays, she dedicated herself to school, excelled in math and science, joined the cheerleading squad, attended football games, and hung out with her friends. But deep down, she longed to dance. Her dance time was so precious that every morning Payal created a daily schedule down to the exact minute that determined when she would study for each subject, when she would go to cheerleading practice, and when she could practice her dance. On the weekends, Payal performed for her community, and she danced with her traditional Indian ensembles. Hard work and determination slowly built up a wall of confidence so thick that words of hate, bullying, or racism no longer penetrated Payal's skin.

However, the hardest time of balancing her dual life always came in the fall. As a member of the cheerleading squad, Payal spent Friday nights at football games, jumping, cartwheeling, and standing at the top of the squad's pyramid. And as soon as the game concluded, she waved goodbye to her friends who were headed off to the postgame party, then tore off her cheerleading uniform, threw on her Indian sari, and drove to the festival of Navratri, where she danced and celebrated with her Indian community, often until two or three o'clock in the morning.

In high school, Payal became the first girl to win the physics award for the top-performing physics student at her high school. She graduated and was admitted into MIT where she majored in operational research, which is a scientific approach to management. And it was at MIT where Payal found her voice. While she was only four foot eleven—about the height of an average sixth grader—Payal had found confidence and focus through dance over the years.

She sought out places in Boston to dance with a traditional Indian group, and when she realized one didn't exist, she decided to start one. During her four years at MIT, Payal found other Indian women to join her dance group. She led rehearsals and choreographed each performance for MIT's cultural shows, often a daunting task considering many of the women had never danced before. This experience taught Payal how to lead, teach, and manage people. And it would go on to change her life.

Payal's First Jobs

After graduating MIT, Payal moved to New York City and took a job at a consulting company. For three years, she made good money, but worked long hours with a predictable schedule, which she didn't care for. After three years, many of her colleagues were planning to attend business school next and were busily studying for the GMAT, the standardized test prospective business school students need to take. Grudgingly, Payal joined the same plan. She purchased GMAT study books and researched different business schools, often questioning if this was the right future for her.

One day while Payal was walking to work, she noticed some excitement across the street and crossed the road to investigate. It turned out to be auditions for the hit television show *So You Think You Can Dance*. Payal's eyes lit up. She quickly pulled out her phone, called her boss, and pretended to be sick. Payal spent the rest of the day in line for the auditions and spontaneously performed for the producers. She didn't make the TV show, but it wasn't all a loss. Payal had seen the day as a sign. Her future was meant for dance.

That evening, Payal threw away her GMAT study books and quit her job shortly thereafter. She took a new position in the music industry at Warner Musical Group and decided to start an Indian dance troupe in New York City, just as she had done at MIT.

When Payal was 25 years old, she opened the Sa Dance Troupe. It was a daunting task, but Payal loved the challenge. She recruited dancers and led rehearsals after work, often until 11:00 PM. She choreographed each performance, managed the group's stage and costume needs, and booked performances on stages across New York City. And when many of her friends started traveling and taking exotic vacations, Payal stayed behind, hustling every extra minute she had to make Sa Dance Troupe a success.

Before long, the Sa Dance Troupe was performing to sold-out audiences in New York City. Audiences fell in love with the emotion, passion, and beauty of the Indian culture. One Sunday morning, Payal woke up to find a picture of herself and the Sa Dance Troupe on the cover of the *New York Times* arts section!

The Sa Dance Troupe brought happiness back into Payal's life. It also brought happiness back in the lives of the other dancers in her troupe. Payal began realizing that people, in general, want to spend their free time doing the things that make them happy, just as dance made her happy. She started to wonder if there was a way to blend her passion for dance with her business expertise.

Misty Copeland, A Dance Pioneer

Misty Copeland started dancing ballet when she was 13 years old in 1995. At the time, she was living in a motel with her mother and five siblings. By 1996 Misty had won a national competition and was named the best dancer in California. She turned professional the next year, and in 2015 she became the first African American principal dancer for the American Ballet Theatre, one of the leading ballet companies in the United States.

The Idea

In the summer of 2010, Payal flew to San Francisco for a friend's birthday party. It was there that she met dozens of entrepreneurs.

Each one was starting a company, launching a new app, or had created a platform around their passion. Payal thought this sounded amazing and asked, "You do this full time?" The concept of entrepreneurship lit up Payal's mind. There must be a way for her to start a business around her passion for dance.

Two days later, Payal was back in New York City and eager to find a ballet class as part of her dance training. She brought ballet clothes to work, and when work was done, she started searching online for a ballet class. She pulled up several locations, read the different teachers' techniques, compared various types of ballet classes, tried syncing class schedules with subway times, and soon became overwhelmed. "This is a disaster!" she said aloud as she realized two hours had gone by and she had missed most of the classes. *There must be a better way to find a ballet class*, she thought. And then it hit her. Perhaps technology could put all the class information in one place.

Payal researched how companies like OpenTable brought a traditional reservation process to an easy-to-use app. The idea was scalable—or easy to grow. There was a need out there. And in the end, Payal knew she'd be helping people find an activity that they loved. She continued working at Warner Music Group, but spent evenings and weekends fleshing out her business idea. She called it Dabble, thinking people would dabble in different activities. Payal's friends liked the idea, which fueled her desire to explore it further. Soon, it was all she could think of.

In 2010 Payal drove to her parent's house for Thanksgiving and spent the weekend there. She sat them down and excitedly explained how Dabble would allow people to easily find and book classes of any type of activity. Her parents listened attentively, then noticed a change of attitude when Payal talked about returning to work on Monday morning. Instead of being excited like she had when she shared the Dabble idea, Payal became depressed and deflated. Payal's mother looked her daughter in the eyes and asked, "Why don't you quit?"

Those four words meant the world to Payal. Despite everything that her parents had risked and worked for to provide Payal with a safe, stable future, they supported her passion for dance and her entrepreneurial drive. Payal hugged her parents, knowing that having their blessing to pursue her entrepreneurial dream was exactly what she needed to take the next step.

Payal quit her job in January 2011. On the day she announced her resignation, the vice chairman of the company, a man named Michael Fleischer, asked to speak to Payal. Nervous, she stepped into his office and wondered what he was going to say. But her nerves turned to excitement when Michael said, "Tell me more about your idea." Payal's described what Dabble was and how it would solve the problem of booking classes. Michael listened patiently, then smiled. He thought it was brilliant and wanted to invest. He handed her a check for $10,000. "It's the scariest day of my life," Payal remembered of that moment. "I'm about to quit my job and I walk out with a $10,000 check."

Growing It

Payal quickly raised $500,000 to start her business. Many of her early investors were friends and colleagues who had seen her juggle working a full-time job and successfully running Sa Dance Troupe. But it wasn't all good news. First, Payal had to change the name from Dabble because a company already existed with that name. She chose Classtivity—a name she created from the words—Class and Activity.

Classtivity's business plan at the time was to gather all the information from various of classes—from fitness classes to art classes to photography classes—in one spot, like a search engine. But on the day of Classtivity's launch, not one person reserved a class. In fact, it took 10 days before the first person signed up for a class! Payal was quickly burning through her $500,000 and needed to make a hard decision. She still believed there was something to her idea, but Classtivity was not it.

Payal knew where she had to go: the fitness studios. She took classes in yoga, spinning, and weight training. She got sweaty and stinky in class then talked to studio owners afterward. She wanted to know what their challenges and struggles were. She talked to the customers about which classes they enjoyed and what kept them coming back.

Two things became very clear: studio owners' biggest challenge was getting new customers into their studio for the first time, and then keeping them there. Customers' biggest challenge was figuring out how to take a variety of classes but in a cost-effective way. Determined to figure it out, Payal had a new idea.

Instead of just *showing* users all the classes possible that they could take—which was very overwhelming—Payal decided to offer customers a great deal to *attend* classes. In June 2013, Payal launched a new subscription service called the Classtivity Passport. For $49, customers could take up to 10 fitness classes over the course of 30 days, but not the same class twice. That meant one day you could take a yoga class at one studio, the next day you could take a spinning class at a different studio, and then you could take a lifting class at a different gym the following day. Some people signed up, but Payal still had work to do.

Next, Payal created Classtivity ClassPass—a monthly subscription where users paid $99 a month and could go to any 10 classes and could go back to their favorite classes up to three times. This was a great deal because most classes cost at least $20 a session. Now, lots of people signed up.

Payal knew immediately that ClassPass was a better product and a better name. Plus, no one could spell Classtivity—they kept mixing up the *i*'s and *t*'s. She renamed her company ClassPass, and off it went. But growing her company meant she had to raise more money. Payal often found herself in a room pitching her idea and— just as she had felt as a young girl in school—she felt different. She was an Indian woman under five feet tall. Most of the time, the room was filled with White men who were at least a foot taller than she. But *unlike* Payal as a young girl, adult Payal was never intimidated. She never doubted herself. In fact, despite being the shortest person in the room, Payal always felt like the tallest. Her life of being different had trained her for these moments: "I knew I was smart, had passion, and could work hard. I always had confidence." It was confidence she had built up through her years of dancing, years of leading, and years of learning who she was.

Payal Kadakia and ClassPass Today

Payal's journey of living a dual life has come together in unison. She confidently tells people, "I'm a dancer and a businesswoman. I am short, but I am powerful. I'm Indian, but I'm American."

ClassPass now employees hundreds of people in multiple cities. The company has created a points system where users can redeem points for specific classes, and that seems to be the perfect solution for both customers and studio owners.

Most recently, Payal realized that as the chief executive officer, or CEO, she was spending more time managing people versus doing what she was good at: creating solutions to problems. She stepped down as CEO and handed the reins over to one of her colleagues. "The CEO title was defining me from what I was good at and wanted to do," Payal explained. With the recent freedom from the CEO title, Payal has refocused on discovering best ways to grow ClassPass internationally and tackle problems such as COVID-19, which kept customers out of studios. But most important, Payal has never stopped dancing. "I kept dancing because it gave me clarity, helped me guide my decisions, helped me connect me to the product."

In 2020, just 10 years after Payal's first idea, ClassPass was valued at $1 billion. But it's not the money that makes Payal proud. "I felt like I was put on this earth to do this," she explained. Her passion for dance, for staying active, and for staying fit allowed Payal to bring ClassPass to others. And her parents who fled India to give their children a better future couldn't be prouder. "I think that's the most reward[ing] part of this," Payal mentions with a smile.

Follow Payal Kadakia and ClassPass Online:

Website: https://classpass.com/

Instagram: @payal and @classpass

Twitter: @PayalKadakia and @classpass

Facebook: ClassPass

6

Alli Webb: Drybar

How does a quiet girl who struggled in school grow up to create a $200 million company with 4,000 employees, all from an idea that changed the *entire* hair industry? She has her curly hair and a drive to make women look beautiful to thank.

Alli Webb was born with naturally curly hair—*really* naturally curly hair! As early as six years old, she begged her mom, a beautiful woman who was always pulled together with style, to blow out her hair because Alli hated the way it frizzed up and wildly pointed in just about every direction. And while Alli couldn't articulate it back then, she knew that having slick, smooth hair made her feel happier, better, and more confident—even as a little girl.

When Alli was a young girl, her family moved from Long Island, New York, to Boca Raton, Florida. Her parents were entrepreneurs and opened a clothing store called Flip's. Year after year, Alli watched how her parents ran a business. They treated their customers with kindness and respect. They took great pride in the way their store was designed. They carefully displayed products with thought and care. And they developed creative ways to keep their customers happy. For instance, every morning, her father brought fresh coffee and bagels into Flip's, knowing that if customers were comfortable and enjoying free food, they would shop longer.

Alli's older brother Michael ran the show at home. He was an overachiever, enjoyed school, and received excellent grades. And while he sometimes found trouble with his friends, Alli's parents considered Michael to be a leader, with a bright future ahead of him. Alli, on the other hand, was the opposite of her older brother. A quiet kid, she considered herself to have grown up in the background of the family. She enjoyed the Florida sunshine and playing with her other tomboy friends, but never got in trouble like her big brother. Alli followed the rules at home and at school and felt comfort in watching her brother overachieve at life, rather than doing it herself. She often struggled at school and had a hard time finding a subject that excited her. Once in a while, she overheard her parents worrying, "What in the world is Alli going to do with her life?"

Alli attended Olympic Heights Community High School and went through her teenage years a bit lost. Her friends, one by one, started discovering their passions and what they wanted to do with their lives. Alli again felt more like an observant bystander, taking it all in rather than knowing what she wanted for herself. "I felt lost!" she recalls. Alli also felt pressure from her family and friends to go to college, so she attended Florida State University. But traditional college classes didn't excite her either, and she stopped showing up for class. Instead, over time Alli became more and more curious about hair, the hair industry, and fashion. She had dreams that she might become a stylist for celebrities one day or maybe work at fashion shows. Finally, it came to her where she needed to be— New York City.

Alli's First Jobs

Alli had finally figured out who she was and what she wanted to do with her life. She brought her parents together and told them that college was not the right place for her. Instead, she wanted to go to beauty school.

"Beauty school?" her mother gasped. "Why would you want to go to beauty school and cut old ladies' hair all day?" Alli calmed her parents down, explaining that she didn't want to work at the hair salon in town where the average customer was 70 years old. No, she wanted to go to New York City and train under the talented John Sahag—the most famous and influential hair stylist in the city.

But first Alli needed to attend beauty school. She walked into the first day of beauty school and a wave of relief set in. She was finally content. "These are my people!" she said aloud. Alli learned all about styling different types of hair. She moved to New York City and, just as she planned, she got a job working for John Sahag. But Alli was a rookie in the hair industry and not yet allowed to cut and color the customer's hair. Instead, she was given two jobs: wash and blow dry their hair. That was it.

Alli loved it. She loved working with different people, different hair types, and different styles. She had tricks, too, that customers seemed to adore. For example, she always turned the chair around so the customers couldn't see their hair until she was finished. Then, just as it was perfect, Alli twirled the chair back in front of the mirror for the big reveal. It was her favorite part of the job!

Time passed, and Alli started to feel pressure from society that maybe working in a hair salon wasn't good enough. Many of her friends worked in marketing, advertising, and public relations, so one day she quit her job. John pulled her aside and said, "Are you sure you want to do this? You are very talented at working with hair." It was the ultimate compliment from the best in the business but—like always—Alli had made up her mind, and there was no stopping her.

Alli took a new job at a public relations firm that helped companies get their stories out into media. She learned how to write well, pitch ideas, and talk to the media. But she now had a new goal in mind. Get married and have kids. And just like that, Alli switched gears in life.

Alli fell in love with a man named Cameron Webb. They moved to Los Angeles and before long, Alli and Cameron had two sons named Grant and Kit. But now, Alli was bored.

The Idea

Alli missed hair. She missed talking to customers, working on their hair, and making women look great. Occasionally, Alli would blow-dry a friend's hair for an event or big business meeting. It always looked fabulous and word started to spread: Alli was exceptional at blow-drying and styling women's hair.

One day while the dryer hummed and the hair spray flowed, a friend made a comment: "Alli, you should start a business doing this. Women would pay you to make them look this great." At first, she didn't believe her friend. But the idea lingered for a few days... *Would women really pay her to blow-dry and style their hair?* She had to find out.

Alli posted an announcement on a website for new moms announcing who she was—a former New York City hair stylist—and that she would drive to customer's houses to give stylish blow-dries to young moms while their babies napped. Her fee was only $40, an easy number, she figured, because most women had two twenties in their wallet. It cost significantly less than an upscale hair salon, which might run $200 to $300. Just like that, Alli's calendar was booked. She had found a hole in the market, and women loved what she had to offer.

Every morning, she hopped into her 2001 Nissan Xterra, dropped Grant and Kit off at school, then raced from house to house doing as many hair blowouts as she could fit in. At the end of the day, she raced back to pick her kids up at school and was home for homework and dinner.

Cameron watched curiously as the popularity of Alli's mobile styling business continued to grow. He created a cute website for her, and, almost overnight, online requests for appointments piled up. Before long, Alli had more customers than she had hours in a day. She was on to something and started to think there was more to this blow-dry idea.

Cameron (who was bald!) wanted to help Alli grow her business. He was very creative and knew how to create a logo, website, and marketing strategy. Alli also decided she needed someone to handle more of the behind-the-scenes financial side of the business. And she knew exactly whom she needed to call.

Alli approached her older brother Michael, who was working in New York City at the time. "I have an idea to start a business that just washes and blow dries women's hair," Alli explained. "And I want you to join our team."

Michael, like Cameron, was also bald and responded, "I don't get it. You don't want to cut hair? You don't want to color hair. All you want to do is blow-dry it?"

Alli smiled and confidently answered, "Yep! That's all I want to do." She explained how she had created a thriving mobile blow-drying business among the members of the Los Angeles mom group. Women didn't want to cut or color their hair all the time, she explained. But they did want a professional to blow it out, giving them that beautiful, confident look that Alli had also longed for since she was six years old. Her customers would come to her salon before big events, small events, before work or date night, or just to feel good. And the price would be affordable—somewhere between $40 and $50. Michael thought for a minute, realized his little sister was a genius, and declared, "I'm in."

Alli's Entrepreneurship Tip: Recognize your strengths and bring in people who know things you don't. It sounds simple, but my best advice is to know you can't possibly do it all. You can't be good at everything. You need help from people you respect and trust.

The three founders divided up the to-do list. Alli would run the store. She would figure out all the products and hairstyling equipment and create the different hairstyles offered. Cameron would create the website and marketing plan. And Michael would round out the team with his business knowledge and financial experience. To help fund the business, Michael put in $250,000 from his savings and Cameron cashed out his retirement account.

Alli and Michael picked out a location in Brentwood, California—a hip neighborhood near Hollywood and Beverly Hills. They hired an architect who worked with Alli to make her vision a reality. Alli knew exactly what she wanted. It must look like and feel like a bar. There would be fun, hip music booming from the speakers and chick flicks with subtitles playing on the televisions. Chargers for phones and laptops graced each station along with a swivel chair. Alli chose the products and brushes, noting, "I didn't want stylists to bring in their own products—I wanted a uniform look, for all of our products, tools, and brushes to be the same. I wanted our clients to be Drybar clients and to come in for the Drybar experience." Finally, Alli used techniques that she had learned from John Sahag's salon in New York City and from blowing out women's hair in their living rooms. Alli insisted stylists work on their customers' hair with the mirror at the clients' backs. "I didn't want clients staring at themselves in the mirror. I wanted clients to let the stress go," she explained. Once the hair was perfect, stylists twirled their customers around for the big reveal.

The salon's color scheme blended white and charcoal-gray color tones with pops of a buttercup yellow throughout. The stylists were hired and trained. Drybar was ready to launch.

Lyda Newman, Inventor of the Modern Hairbrush

The origins of the first hairbrush are unknown, but the first modern hairbrush was invented by Lyda Newman, an African American girl who was living in New York City in 1898. Lyda was just 13 years old and had a job working on women's hair, but found the bristles of the traditional brush didn't work well on Black people's hair. Her invention included several improvements. First, she replaced the animal hair on brushes with synthetic bristles, which were stronger and lasted longer. Second, she spaced the bristles out so they would be more efficient at untangling hair. Third, Lyda added an air chamber, which allowed airflow to run in between the bristles, and a compartment to catch dandruff. Lyda Newman was the third Black woman ever to receive a patent and went on to be an advocate for women's rights. She became one of the organizers of the African American branch of the Woman Suffrage Party.

Growing It

Drybar launched in February 2010. The morning of opening day, Alli was petrified. Would anyone show up? She had hired six stylists and eight empty chairs were ready to go, but she couldn't shake her nerves. Then Alli pulled up to the salon and her mouth dropped. "The day we opened . . . there was a line out the door!" she remembers. "The ladies were so excited and instantly loved the idea of getting a great blowout, in a beautiful space and at an affordable price." From that moment, Alli knew she was on to something.

Originally, Alli hoped to do 30 to 40 blowouts a day. She ended up doing 80 a day. Women lined up to get a time slot and became angry when they couldn't get in. She had solved a problem no one else had figured out before her—how to give women gorgeous and affordable blowouts in a fabulous setting. For six months, Alli worked day and night without a day off. It was time to open a second store. And it didn't stop there. Demand for Drybar store kept growing. So, she opened a third store, then a fourth store, and more!

Life was crazy and nonstop for Alli. She was raising her two boys, opening stores, and training stylists day after day. She recounts, "We learned pretty quickly that we could not do this on our own and needed to hire people with much more experience than ourselves to help us scale the business."

In 2013 Michael and Cameron thought it was time to hire someone else to take over as the CEO. But Alli wasn't so sure. She worried that a new CEO could change the culture of the business she had carefully built. She hesitantly agreed to meet a man named John Heffner. At their first meeting, Alli and Michael saw a six-foot-five man wearing a polished business suit and carrying a briefcase approach them. Alli turned to her brother and stated, "Hell, no. This is *not* the guy." But Michael insisted that they go through with the meeting and talk with him. John, they learned, had worked in the beauty industry before. He had helped other entrepreneurs take their business to the next level. He was professional, but also very respectful of the culture Alli had built and wanted to preserve it, not change it. Alli and Michael left the meeting, looked each other in the eye, and smiled. This, in fact, was their guy.

John helped Drybar expand by taking over fundraising and managing the business, which meant Alli could spend her time focusing on the salons and what her customers needed. She created almost a dozen different hairstyles that were available in every salon. She came up with fun, identifiable names, such as the Manhattan, a sleek and smooth look; the Straight Up, a straight blow-dry with a little bit of body; the Mai Tai, a messy beach hairstyle; and the Cosmo, with lots of loose curls. She added styles for girls with names like the Shirley Temple, and started selling hair products, hair dryers, and straightening irons. From 2013 to 2020, the company grew from a handful of locations to over 100 locations; almost every state had at least one Drybar location. Soon, Drybar sales topped $100 million, then $200 million! Alli's business grew to employ 3,000 people and sell thousands of products at retailers such as Nordstrom, Sephora, and Ulta.

Alli's Advice for Entrepreneurs: Don't let perfect stand in the way of progress. Don't be afraid to take a leap of faith on an idea you have! Just be sure to surround yourself with the right partners, who have the skills you lack.

Alli Webb and Drybar Today

Today, Alli continues to run Drybar, raise her two teenage boys, launch a new massage business called Squeeze, and produce a podcast called *Raising the Bar*. She continues to worry about customer service, a trait that most likely dates back to her days as a child and watching her parents treat every single customer with care and respect. She explained, "One of the biggest challenges has been how to maintain the same level of client service at 100 locations that we had at 10. It's really hard. And is what keeps me up at night." But she has faith that the family-like atmosphere she has created makes all of her employees feel like an important part of Drybar.

Alli can often be found speaking to young adults at colleges and high schools, and inspiring others to follow their dreams and pursue their ideas. Because you never know when that naturally curly hair you hate, might change the world.

Follow Alli Webb and Drybar Online:

Website: www.drybarshops.com

Instagram: @alliwebb and @thedrybar

Twitter: @theDrybar

Facebook: Drybar

Part III: Science and Technology

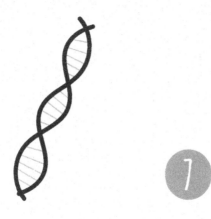

Anne Wojcicki: 23andMe

23andMe's first office was located on Shorebird Lane, just down the road from Google, the company that Anne's husband at the time, Sergey Brin, had cofounded. Google was a thriving work environment, and was also famous for feeding its employees very well. With a wide range of cafés and food options, Googlers ate for free!

Anne often rode her bike over to the Google campus to grab herself a free lunch. Soon, she was picking up lunch for a few of her employees, too. One day, Anne was craving burritos, and, knowing that Google had a delicious burrito café on campus, she headed over to Google. After ordering 10 burritos, Anne carefully balanced them in her arms, but struggled as she tried to open the door to leave the café. Suddenly, the door swung open and there stood Eric Schmidt, the new CEO of Google, and Steve Jobs, the founder and CEO of Apple!

Eric looked at Anne with her arms full of burritos and asked, "What are you doing?" Anne stuttered a bit, then answered, "Uh . . . just getting some lunch?" Steve Jobs, who had just launched the new iPhone, looked at Anne, ignored the burritos overflowing from her arms and instead asked, "Do you want to see the iPhone?" Anne smiled at Steve and answered, "Yes!"

Anne Wojcicki (pronounced whoa-JIT–skee) grew up in sunny California on the campus of Stanford University. Her father, Stanley, was a physics professor and the chairman of Stanford's physics department. Her mother, Esther, was an award-winning journalism teacher who taught at the local high school.

Despite their successful careers as adults, neither of Anne's parents had had an easy childhood. In 1949, when Stanley was 12 years old, his family fled Poland after the Communists took control of the country. Esther's parents were Orthodox Jews who immigrated to New York from Russia in the 1920s, and struggled with poverty for many years. But despite these hardships, both parents persevered and created successful lives for themselves in education. And they expected the same from their children.

Stanley and Esther raised their three daughters—Susan, Janet, and Anne—in a tight-knit family. They continuously preached the lesson that there is always more to learn. Anne remembered that "I would write a paper and then I'd give it to my mom, and it would come back solid red, and she'd be like, 'You can either turn this in and you'll get a C or a D, or you can rewrite it. And then you rewrite it. 'Well, now it's better. Now it's a B.' And you want to rewrite it again."

Anne was the youngest of the three sisters. The Wojcickis lived modestly, which taught their daughters how to save money and not crave material goods. They encouraged free thinking, bravery, and often reminded the girls, "Don't be afraid if someone disagrees with you." "My parents really looked at us always as like mini adults," Anne explained. "I think the one thing that my parents really did is they gave us a taste of freedom. And they encouraged it. They encouraged us to find our passions, they weren't controlling. . . . We were just very supported, but we were really encouraged to, you know, be creative and to be independent."

As a young girl, Anne loved sports. She naturally took risks, enjoyed adventure, and became comfortable with learning from her failures at an early age. But when her parents encouraged her to play tennis, she put her foot down. Anne had little interest in tennis and instead found figure skating. This was one of the few times that Anne's parents did not support their daughter and continued to push tennis on the young girl. They even told her that if she wanted to ice-skate instead of play tennis, she would have to pay for her own lessons and equipment. So, Anne did.

Anne traded babysitting for skating lessons and won fundraising competitions each year to help pay for new ice skates when she outgrew her old ones. Over time, Anne's passion for figure skating evolved into a love for ice hockey. She attended Gunn High School in Palo Alto, California; played hockey; and wrote for the school newspaper. After graduating high school, Anne attended Yale University in Hartford, Connecticut, where she majored in biology and played varsity hockey. While at Yale she was thrilled with the intellectual environment but admittedly became a bit of a snob in the academic world, only wanting to focus on the subjects that fascinated her, like biology.

Anne's First Jobs

Anne graduated from Yale in 1996 and took a job as a health care investment analyst on Wall Street. She loved it. Each day, she learned about different companies in health care, how they operated, how they made drugs, how they made money, and which companies to invest in and not invest in.

Meanwhile, Anne's sister Susan was working at a company called Intel and had bought a house in Menlo Park, California. To help pay the mortgage, she rented her garage to two men who had just left Stanford to start a new company. Their names were Larry Page and Sergey Brin. And their company was called Google.

When Anne returned home to California, she visited Susan and, from the other room, could see Larry and Sergey coding on their computers until late at night. Anne sometimes said to her sister, "It's really weird that you have these guys in the other room coding while we're doing the dishes." Turns out, these guys were on to something big, and while Google grew at lightning speed, Anne became especially close with Sergey.

Anne Wojcicki and Sergey Brin

Anne and Sergey started dating shortly after they met and got married on a beach in 2007. They invited guests to a remote location in the Bahamas, flying them in on a private jet. For the ceremony, Anne wore a white bathing suit, and Sergey wore a black bathing suit. They swam out to a sandbar and took their vows in the ocean.

Anne and Sergey have two children named Benji and Chloe. The couple divorced in 2015 but continue to remain friends and run their foundation that supports nonprofits in research and science. They have donated more than $150 million to the Michael J. Fox Foundation, which focuses on Parkinson's disease.

As Anne got to know Larry and Sergey, she often shared her viewpoints about the health care industry with them. She complained about how doctors, hospitals, and pharmaceutical companies only made money when people were sick. She showed them examples of how the health care industry was good at monetizing illness, but not wellness. She argued that the health-care system was not always doing the right thing for the consumer. And she complained that 90 percent of everything in biotech fails.

Anne's negative viewpoints were also a product of how she was raised. Her mother, Esther, was very skeptical of the health care industry, and for good reason. When Esther was a little girl, her 18-month-old brother got into the family medicine cabinet and swallowed an entire bottle of aspirin. The family, who was very poor, rushed Esther's little brother to a hospital but didn't have any money or medical insurance for care. So they were turned away. They went to another hospital but were turned away again. By the time they found a hospital that would take Esther's brother, the little boy was in critical condition. The next morning, Esther's 18-month-old brother was dead. From that day on, Esther refused to let the medical industry tell her how to take care of herself or her family. In fact, Esther was so forceful with doctors that she often got "fired" from pediatrician's offices for asking too many questions and demanding too many answers.

As Anne rambled on about all the problems in health care industry, Larry listened carefully, then turned to her and said, "Anne, you can either be part of the solution or part of the problem. Right now, you are part of the problem." Larry was right. Anne was part of the problem. And this slap in the face was exactly what she needed to hear.

Letitia Geer, Inventor of the Medical Syringe

Hypodermic syringes are considered one of the most important medical inventions and save lives by delivering medicine safely and effectively. But who invented them? During the late 1800s, several medical innovations came about. In 1844, a physician named Francis Rynd invented the hollow needle able to pierce the skin. In 1853 Charles Pravaz and Alexander Wood developed a hypodermic metal syringe with a needle.

Then in 1899, a woman from New York named Letitia Mumford Geer invented a syringe viable across all medical fields. She patented her invention: "In a hand-syringe the combination of a cylinder, a piston and an operating-rod which is bent upon itself to form a smooth and rigid arm terminating in a handle, which, in its extreme positions, is located within reach of the fingers of the hand which holds the cylinder, thus permitting one hand to hold and operate the syringe." Letitia Geer's one-handed design changed the way doctors deliver medications to patients and forever changed the medical world.

The Idea

Anne had an idea. It was 2006 and she was acutely aware of three trends in the world. One, a genetics revolution was underway, and the cost of finding one's genome had come down significantly. Two, social networking was growing exponentially. Three, crowdsourcing was also a new revolution. Anne wondered, *Could I crowdsource the world's DNA? Could I help figure out what portion of health problems were nature versus nurture? Could I empower consumers to take control of their own health by understanding their genome? Could I create a platform where people could access their genetic information and what diseases they were at risk for?* If it worked, Anne would flip the health care system on its head *and* create a whole new way to do research!

Anne hypothesized that if she collected massive amounts of DNA data, science could make more discoveries and ultimately turn them into new drug therapies. Her goal was to give *consumers* their medical DNA, which could be used in keeping them healthy. She also wanted to work together with scientists and pharmaceutical companies and help them create drugs that work better. This was her time.

In 2006 Anne partnered with Linda Avey and Paul Cusenza to create 23andMe, named after the 23 pairs of chromosomes in a normal human cell. (Paul left the company in 2007; Linda left the company in 2009.)

What Is DNA? What Is a Genome?

DNA is the unique chemical code that guides our growth, development, and health. It's like an instruction book for all living things. DNA is coiled into a shape called the double helix, a structure that looks like a double ladder. The double helix is found within chromosomes, which are located in every normal cell. There are 23 pair of chromosomes in every normal cell. The complete set of DNA's genetic instructions is called a genome. Basically, the genome is a digital code of you. Differences or variants in the DNA can make a difference in how a thing looks or responds to its environment. Some variants can affect your health.

Here's how 23andMe works. First, consumers pay either $99 or $199 for a 23andMe kit. When the kit arrives, it includes a spit tube. The consumer spits in the tube, seals it up, then mails it back to 23andMe. A few weeks later, 23andMe sends the consumer an email with a link to his or her profile that includes one of two reports. The $99 report gives consumers their ancestry report plus dozens of trait reports. That means consumers can see which parts of the world their ancestors came from as well as learn if they are more likely to have traits such as thick hair, obesity, freckles, or even sticky earwax. The $199 report gives consumers their ancestry report and the trait report, as well as a report that shows a genetic link to several diseases. With this report, people can learn if, based on their DNA, they are at a higher risk of getting diseases such as breast cancer, cystic fibrosis, and Parkinson's disease.

So, what happened when 23andMe first launched? Some people signed up, but not many. About 15 kits were sold a day. Anne needed more media attention, so she held "spit parties" all over the country. She invited celebrities, influencers, and the media to spit in a tube and receive their DNA reports. It worked! In 2008, 23andMe's product was named the "Invention of the Year" by *Time* magazine, and sales started to take off. For the next few years, 23andMe continued to grow, exceeding 1 million people in its database.

Then one day in 2013, a letter arrived in the mail. It was from the Food and Drug Administration (FDA). They warned 23andMe must cease marketing of their product immediately. Concerned with the accuracy of 23andMe's health tests, the FDA worried that people might take their test results and chose to do something drastic, such as change their medications without a doctor's guidance or undergo an unnecessary surgery.

Like usual, Anne disagreed. She didn't think she needed approval from the FDA to provide customers with information about their own DNA and potential health risks. For months, Anne tried to figure out how to get around the FDA's regulations and ultimately hit a wall. "You just accept at some point, you're regulated, and there's no Silicon-Valley, 24-hour, easy fix," she explained. "That setback [in 2013] was a challenge to overcome, and I realized we were so focused on the work to instill in our staff about the long-term vision of the company that we didn't look down the path of providing the FDA with our clinical and analytical validity," Anne explained.

For several years, Anne focused on getting back the trust from the FDA and the public. They changed many things within the company and became a regulated company, which Anne thinks ultimately makes 23andMe a better company. In 2015, the FDA began giving approval to 23andMe.

Anne Wojcicki and 23andMe Today

By 2017, 23andMe had 2 million people in their database, and a year later they had had more than 5 million people. By 2021, 23andMe had accumulated 3 billion points of data from over 12 million customers. 23andMe's mission is to help people access, understand, and benefit from the human genome. They have also become the largest genetic study in the world, providing people with important information about what diseases they are more at risk for. They are currently partnering with dozens of pharmaceutical companies to help use the data to create new and effective drugs and treatments.

Anne, who is often called by her nickname "Woj," continues to balance managing 23andMe and raising her two children. Addicted to fitness and health, she wakes up early, kisses her children good morning, throws on some Lululemon shorts and a T-shirt, then rides her bike to work and parks it in the front lobby. At 23andMe's headquarters in Mountain View, California, pink and green balloons float around the office space, and Polaroid photographs of each employee line the wall of the cafeteria. They hang in the order of when the employee joined the company and feature a fun fact about the employee. Anne's fun fact? "I once ate so many carrots that I turned orange and was told not to eat carrots for a year."

When asked if she views herself as successful, she replied, "People tend to look at success and failure as black and white. For me, it's like you're always moving. I come from the science world. You're like an atom. You're constantly vibrating."

Follow Anne Wojcicki and 23andMe Online:

Website: www.23andme.com

Instagram: @annewoj23 and @23andMe

Twitter: @annewoj23 and @23andMe

Facebook: 23andMe

Morgan DeBaun: Blavity

As Morgan headed for the lunch table, she smiled with excitement. The college campus burned with energy and for the first time in her life, she felt part of a community—a Black community. The lunch table, which was only supposed to fit eight people, ended up being surrounded by dozens of Black classmates each day. They came from all over. Some were friends, some were newcomers, some were freshman, some were seniors. Athletes, poets, academics . . . it didn't matter who they were or what their passion was, the lunch table was a place for conversation and community. And the conversation covered just about everything. *How had their class gone that morning? What was their test on that afternoon? Where had they been over the weekend? What had they eaten last night? What new music had just hit? What was going on in politics, the environment, in their hometown, in Hollywood?*

They called it Blavity, a name that combined "Black" and "gravity." It was a name that had been passed down for years by the Black students at Washington University. Blavity was happening at the college campus lunch table, and Morgan wanted to bring it to the world.

Morgan DeBaun was born in 1990 in St. Louis, Missouri. She grew up in a predominately White neighborhood, but her parents always created a home for Morgan and her older brother where they embraced their Blackness. "We had Black Santas, Black Cinderella books, photos of Muhammad Ali and Dr. Martin Luther King Jr. in the house, and attended a Black church," Morgan recalled. But outside of her home and church life, Morgan often felt different. She attended elementary school at a private Catholic school, where she was one of the only Black girls in her grade. It was then that she started to realize the difference between reality and her world.

By the time she reached middle school, Morgan's parents decided she should be surrounded by positive Black role models and more kids who looked like her, so they sent her to a magnet school in the city. Morgan loved it. "The first week I came home and was like, 'Woah, Mom, we gotta practice double Dutch and tonk,'" Morgan remembered. "I spent the majority of my time in middle school learning what true diversity looked like and felt comfortable in my Black identity." For inspiration, Morgan read stories of Maya Angelou and Sojourner Truth. She also learned to express herself through art, jewelry making, pottery, and glassblowing.

When Morgan was in middle school, she stumbled upon a problem. The school had removed candy from all the vending machines and kids were angry. *Kids love candy*, Morgan thought to herself.

They need candy. And they would mostly likely pay a premium for candy where it wasn't available. So Morgan came up with her first business idea. She pooled her savings one weekend and headed to Costco, a wholesale warehouse store that offered large amounts of food at a very low cost. There, Morgan purchased boxes of candy, brought them to her school the next week, and sold the candy for a premium to candy-deprived classmates. She also invented her own dip stick candy by taking the powder mix from Kool Aid and packing it in bags. Morgan eventually got busted by the teachers, and her candy business was shut down. But it was a powerful lesson in running a business, and when Morgan turned 14 her father knew she had a knack for business and started teaching her how to invest her money.

After high school, Morgan attended Washington University in St. Louis, and it was there that she truly found herself. She majored in political science and minored in entrepreneurship and education. A natural leader, Morgan also became the youngest student body president elected at Washington U. While there, Morgan considered becoming a teacher and briefly worked as a student teacher, but quit, feeling that she would not be given enough freedom to teach how she wanted to. Morgan also considered a life in politics but didn't like how money often influences political decisions.

Where Morgan really found herself was during the lunch hour. Each day, Black students from across campus gathered around the lunch table for hours, sharing knowledge, stories, and culture on topics ranging on everything from politics to class discussions to food and culture. They called it Blavity. Morgan used it in a sentence like this: "Blavity was happening at the lunch table." It was synonymous to life at Washington University, one filled with support, challenges, and open communication. In fact, after Morgan graduated, she was surprised to find the word "Blavity" was not used anywhere *but* at Washington University.

Morgan's First Jobs

Morgan graduated near the top of her class in 2012 and headed to Mountain View, California—where Google is also headquartered. She took a good-paying job as a product manager at Intuit. Intuit is a software company that developed products like TurboTax, which helps users do their taxes, and Quicken, which allows users to easily manage their finances.

Morgan appreciated the business lessons she was learning as well as the experience on how to build great technology brands at Intuit. But day after day, she felt disconnected from her colleagues and community. Just as she had sensed in elementary school, she felt constrained because she was one of the few Black people in her work environment. Morgan worried about what she said, how she acted, if she was being polite enough, and how to straighten her curly hair. Trying to fit in was exhausting both mentally and physically. It was lonely as well: "I found myself thinking[,] 'Is this really the world that I want to live in for the rest of my life?'"

The Idea

Morgan longed for the community and warmth of the Blavity lunch table at Washington University and wondered if she could bring that to the world. Other media companies like *Huffington Post* and BuzzFeed already targeted millennials, but nothing was created for Black millennials. Morgan wanted to create a brand people trusted where Black people could tell their own stories, tout their own heroes, and share their own news—as well as explore travel, food, culture, technology, and more. And she knew just what she would call it: Blavity!

Blavity started as a side project, more specifically an email newsletter that shared the "Top 10 Things You Need to Know" and linked readers back to videos from other sources. Morgan continued to work at Intuit while slowly building the foundation for Blavity. She woke at four or five in the morning, worked for two hours, then headed to work. During her lunch break, she'd squeeze in another hour of work on Blavity, then finish off the day at home hunched over her computer trying to create this new media space. The hours were long, and the growth was slow.

Then one day in 2014 Morgan turned on the news. Images of people protesting in her hometown of St. Louis, Missouri, filled the screen. Brought on by the fatal shooting of Michael Brown by a police officer in Ferguson, Missouri, these protests were the headline story. Morgan knew she needed to do something about it: "So, I'm sitting in my cubicle . . . and my city is in turmoil and there's tension and it's being broadcast around the world and what was my contribution to that? Yes, I could have marched in the streets. Yes, I could have flown back to St. Louis, but really my unique contribution and the contribution of our Blavity team was being able to be a platform for people to get the word out about what was happening." It was then that Morgan understood that Blavity was her destiny. "And so at that moment it became apparent like, OK, there is a disconnect for me and also an information [disconnect] that the Black community has in this country because we have not made it a priority to build our own new-age digital media brand that can distribute accurate information and stories that will never get covered anywhere else."

In October 2014, Morgan DeBaun quit her job at Intuit and partnered with Aaron Samuels, Jonathan Jackson, and Jeff Nelson—all classmates from Washington University—to officially launch Blavity.

The Mission Statement for Black Lives Matter:

#BlackLivesMatter was founded in 2013 in response to the acquittal of Trayvon Martin's murderer. Black Lives Matter Global Network Foundation is a global organization in the US, UK, and Canada, whose mission is to eradicate white supremacy and build local power to intervene in violence inflicted on Black communities by the state and vigilantes. By combating and countering acts of violence, creating space for Black imagination and innovation, and centering Black joy, we are winning immediate improvements in our lives.

We are expansive. We are a collective of liberators who believe in an inclusive and spacious movement. We also believe that in order to win and bring as many people with us along the way, we must move beyond the narrow nationalism that is all too prevalent in Black communities. We must ensure we are building a movement that brings all of us to the front.

We affirm the lives of Black queer and trans folks, disabled folks, undocumented folks, folks with records, women, and all Black lives along the gender spectrum. Our network centers those who have been marginalized within Black liberation movements.

We are working for a world where Black lives are no longer systematically targeted for demise.

We affirm our humanity, our contributions to this society, and our resilience in the face of deadly oppression.

The call for Black lives to matter is a rallying cry for ALL Black lives striving for liberation.

Growing It

In order to gain readers and increase engagement, Blavity hired a handful of journalists to write blogs and quickly realized that their readers preferred Blavity's own content rather than content from somewhere else. But in order to hire journalists and content creators, Morgan needed to raise money.

At first, investors said no. Many of them couldn't understand what Blavity was or see Morgan's vision. "You have to remember that a lot of young Black founders, we tend to look a little bit different than your typical pattern and in Silicon Valley, people often engage in pattern matching," Morgan said. "I'm from the Midwest. I don't have a technical degree. I didn't go to Stanford, and this was my first company, so I was [a] first-time founder. My pitches may have sounded differently." But she stuck with it and over time became one of the most significant Black female fundraisers in the world, raising $11 million.

Morgan DeBaun and Blavity Today

Morgan has used the money she raised to expand her company with new brands. She launched 21Ninety, a women's lifestyle brand. She acquired Shadow & Act, a film and television site that focuses on Black talent. She launched a travel website called Travel Noire. Morgan has also founded two annual conferences with the goal of uplifting and empowering the Black community. Summit21 focuses on empowering women of color. Afrotech brings people together for the largest African American tech conference in Silicon Valley. "One of the specific stories that I love that I hear, are people who went [to Afrotech] last year and now nine months pass since the last conference and they're like launching their company or they've got funding from somebody that they met at that conference," Morgan said. On top of running these media companies, Morgan has launched a skin care brand for Black women called M.Roze Essentials.

Black Executives Today

Racial disparities still exist in business. There have only been 19 Black CEOs out of 1,800 CEOs in the history of the Fortune 500. In 2021 there were only five Black CEOs of Fortune 500 Companies: Roz Brewer at Walgreens, Ken Frazier at Merck, René Jones at M&T Bank, Thasunda Brown Duckett at TIAA, and Marvin Ellison at Lowe's. Marvin Ellison was also the CEO of JCPenney, making him the only Black CEO of two Fortune 500 Companies. The first Black CEO of a major US corporation was Clifton Wharton, who became the CEO of TIAA in 1987. Black entrepreneurs also receive less than 1 percent of funding from venture capital firms.

Blavity remains Morgan's bread and butter, and it is the largest media lifestyle brand in the world for Black millennials, featuring the hottest topics of the day. This young entrepreneur and CEO has already done so much in her life, including raising millions of dollars in funding, acquiring multiple companies, and employing dozens of people in Los Angeles, Atlanta, San Francisco, and New York City. Her accomplishments are so impressive that she is one of only 12

Black women to raise over $1 million in venture funding, and she still finds time for her art: "I'll be honest with you, I am proud of myself."

Follow Morgan DeBaun and Blavity Online:

Website: https://blavity.com/

Instagram: @MorganDeBaun and @blavity

Twitter: @MorganDeBaun and @Blavity

Facebook: Blavity

Jasmine Crowe: Goodr

Jasmine Crowe was born to volunteer. As a child, she collected cans for food drives, and as an adult she volunteered at food kitchens and homeless shelters. One June afternoon, Jasmine joined a group of volunteers to pass out bags of food at a local food pantry in Atlanta, Georgia. Jasmine arrived hopeful and excited, but when she checked in for her shift, she was assigned to the Weight Watcher Ding Dongs.

Weight Watcher Ding Dongs? Jasmine asked herself. *What kind of food was that to feed hungry people?* Jasmine was instructed to place one box of Ding Dongs into each paper bag. She took her place, then looked at the long line of hungry individuals waiting patiently for a bag of food they couldn't afford. As she assessed the assembly line of food items they would receive, a wave of anger passed over her. Here was what was going into that bag:

two 20-ounce Diet Snapples
one gallon BBQ sauce
one bag kettle potato chips

one box superhero-shaped macaroni noodles

one box of breakfast bars

one can of refried beans

one can of corn

one can of sweet peas

one box of french-fried green onions

and of course, the Ding Dongs she had been assigned to.

What on earth are we doing here? Jasmine asked herself. There wasn't a single meal that could be made from this random concoction of food items. She knew there was a difference between providing *food* and providing *meals*. From that day, Jasmine decided she would dedicate her life to feeding the hungry with real, healthy meals.

Jasmine Crowe grew up on a military base with her family. Her mom worked a full-time job, put herself through undergraduate college, and received a master's degree, all while raising Jasmine and her sister. She helped Jasmine understand that hard work makes dreams come true.

Overall, Jasmine had a good childhood and kept busy with gymnastics classes and track meets. When Jasmine was seven, their family took a trip to Washington, DC. Jasmine's young eyes couldn't believe the number of homeless people living on the streets. She asked her father who they were, where they lived, and what they ate. Jasmine's father explained as best he could why some people were

Jasmine Crowe

homeless and took the moment to reinforce the importance of giving back to those in need.

Giving back was an important part of growing up in Jasmine's family: "I definitely have to give a lot of credit to my parents, especially my father. He was always a mentor and he worked with the Big Brothers Big Sisters program. As recently as two weeks ago we found a newspaper article about my dad and his mentoring of children at the military base where we grew up. Those kids actually just found him on Facebook and told him how much of a difference he made, saying they talk about him all the time."

Jasmine graduated North Carolina Central University in 2005 and received her master of business administration (MBA) from the University of Phoenix in 2007. Armed with a good education and a desire to give back, Jasmine was ready to change the world.

Mary Engle Pennington, "The Ice Woman"

When Mary Engle Pennington graduated from college in 1892, she was denied a bachelor's degree because of her gender and instead awarded a certificate of proficiency. But that didn't deter her from changing the food industry and becoming the most important person in the world in food safety. Mary went on to earn a PhD in chemistry, worked for the US Department of Agriculture, and was named the chief of Food Research Lab in 1908. While there, Mary completely changed the procedures for food safety, realizing that perishable foods like dairy, eggs, poultry, and fish, could not be processed, stored, or shipped like other foods. Thanks to her efforts and her work to create the 1906 Pure Food and Drug Act, grocery stores today now include aisles of refrigeration and freezer space to keep food cold and safe from contamination. Mary was inducted into the National Inventors Hall of Fame in 2018, 66 years after her death.

Jasmine's First Jobs

Right out of graduate school, Jasmine bounced between several jobs, allowing herself to gain work experience and figure out what it was that she wanted to do with her life. She worked as an enrollment counselor at University of Phoenix, a worldwide educational consultant, and a public relations and social media marketing consultant, as well as working on admissions recruitment and diversity initiatives at Phoenix School of Law. In her spare time, she volunteered at food pantries and shelters because nothing gave her more joy than giving back, just as her father had taught her at a young age.

In 2009 Jasmine was living in Phoenix and joined an organization called Once A Month Church where they would gather in a park, specifically choosing places where homeless men and women slept. On the first day, Jasmine's eyes were opened to what homelessness and hunger really looked like: "I remember the first time I went with [a friend] to feed people and there were all kinds of people helping us with the setup. I thought they were volunteers like myself, but when it came time to feed people, I saw them getting in line. It opened my eyes to the fact that we don't always know what hunger and homelessness look like. Here I was thinking these folks were volunteers but, in fact, they were homeless themselves."

Four years later, Jasmine moved to Atlanta, Georgia. New to the city, she approached an area where hundreds of homeless people gathered. It was painful for Jasmine to watch people eating off the dirty ground. She wondered what they were eating. She wondered how hungry they were. She wondered where they got their food. And she wondered who was helping them: "Something shook me to my core, and I was so moved at that moment, that I knew I had to do something."

The Idea

In 2013 Jasmine created an event called Sunday Soul. She picked locations in alleyways and under bridges where homeless people tended to gather. She rented tables, chairs, and linens, then set them up like a large restaurant in these locations. She decorated the tables with flowers and menus. She set up speakers that filled the air with the soulful rhythms of Aretha Franklin, Marvin Gaye, and the Jackson 5. And on October 20, 2013, Jasmine served her first meal to a group of homeless individuals, a wholesome course of spaghetti, corn, garlic bread, and salad. As over 100 homeless people dined in dignity, each guest talked, ate, and momentarily forgot their troubles.

Over the next three years, Jasmine expanded Sunday Soul to other cities, including New Orleans, Baltimore, and Washington, DC, and her crowds grew to over 400 homeless people a meal. Then one day, a video of Sunday Soul went viral on Facebook. As Jasmine scrolled through the comments, she noticed the same question kept popping up: "Which restaurant had donated the food?" The answer was none. Not one restaurant had donated the food. And *that* was Jasmine's light-bulb moment.

People Living in Food-Insecure Households

According to Feeding America (www.feedingamerica. org), 35.2 million people lived in food-insecure households in 2019. But in 2020 this number grew to 42 million due to COVID-19. This number includes 13 million children who are food insecure. Every community in the country has families who face hunger but rates of food insecurity are higher among African American, Latino, and Native American families.

Jasmine started to research food waste, and what she found was shocking. Between 1970 and 2017, food waste had more than doubled. Over 72 billion pounds of food was thrown out each year, mostly from grocery stores and restaurants. That was enough wasted food to fill an NFL football stadium every single day. Jasmine dug further and discovered that 27 percent of waste in landfills is food.

As this food rots, it releases methane gas, a big contributor to global climate change.

Jasmine began talking with restaurant owners to confirm whether this information was accurate. She asked what they did with their extra food at the end of the night. They all answered the same thing: they threw it away! Every single night, massive amounts of good food went into the dumpster. One evening, Jasmine saw a hungry man digging through a restaurant dumpster looking for a meal.

Jasmine already knew that 821 million people worldwide went hungry every day, about one in nine people. And 42 million people were hungry in the United States, including 13 million children. She wondered, *What if these two issues—food waste and hunger—could literally solve each other's problem?*

Food Waste Facts

According to the Economic Research Service of the US Department of Agriculture, each person wastes approximately 290 pounds of food per year, or 0.8 pounds per day. Meat, poultry, fish, vegetables, and dairy products account for 68 percent of the annual loss.

In 2017 Jasmine tested her idea at a pitch competition called Spark Prize in Atlanta. She explained how she had an idea to help children eat three meals a day. And how to reduce food waste and pollution. Jasmine won the competition and $15,000 in prize money. With it, she officially launched Goodr, stating "At Goodr, we believe that hunger isn't a scarcity issue. It's a logistics issue."

Goodr created an app that works like this: each day, restaurants take an inventory of the food at their place of business. At the end of the day, they click on the items that remain, and which would be thrown out. Once the quantity is logged in, a local driver picks up the food, packs it into a van, and immediately delivers it to nonprofits where people in need are fed. Within minutes, hungry people receive delicious meals, food that helps them survive and is good for them. In addition, the place of business that donates the food receives a tax benefit for their donation. The overall business idea is a win-win situation. Landfills end up with less food waste, and therefore produce less pollution. And hungry people get fed. One reporter called it an "UberEats in reverse"!

Jasmine's efforts hit the media circuits, and restaurants started signing up. Super Bowl LIII also partnered with Goodr. And with the extra food, Jasmine created even more opportunities like pop-up grocery stores where healthy food was free to those who needed it. Goodr went even further, educating people on how to prepare healthy meals. They handed out free samples of wholesome meals and passed out recipe cards that explained how to cook it.

But it wasn't all easy. Jasmine needed to raise money to make her vision a reality, and most investors she spoke with just didn't get it: "It took almost 200 meetings, hearing no a lot of times. I would get these emails that would say, 'Closing the loop.' or, 'Following up.' I would just know this fund is going to say no, or they're going to deny me. Sure enough, it would always be a denial."

She not only heard no from investors but also was told "What a bad idea!" "Everyone that said, 'She won't be successful. This won't work. We're not going to back her. We're not going to invest in her.' They keep me motivated to prove them wrong." This type of feedback was defeating. "There was a lot of times when I was the only person who believed in my business. Even my parents, I love them to death, but they are workers. They were not entrepreneurs. So, there were times that they said, 'I don't know if this is going to work. Maybe you should get a job.' But I continued to believe in myself." Jasmine's drive to end hunger and help lower food waste was stronger than her temptation to quit. And she didn't quit.

Capital Funding Fact

In 2018 only 3 percent of venture capital funding went to women-led companies. And according to ProjectDiane, less than 1 percent of venture capital funding went to women of color. Despite these realities, companies with at least one female founder outproduce all-male companies by 63 percent.

But there's good news! In 2021 there were 12.3 million women-owned businesses, and there are 114 percent more female entrepreneurs than there were 20 years ago. Plus, 64 percent of new women-owned businesses were started by women of color in 2020.

Jasmine Crowe and Goodr Today

To date, Jasmine has raised over $2.7 million. She has partnered with local restaurants as well as big corporations, including Atlanta's Hartsfield Jackson Airport, SAP, the National Football League, the Georgia World Congress Center, and Netflix. Jasmine has delivered over 2 million meals to people in need. She has kept over 2.2 million pounds of food from filling up the earth's landfills. And she has reduced over 1.3 million pounds of carbon emissions. This fearless entrepreneur followed her passion to help people even when everyone, including her own parents, doubted her. Jasmine Crowe continues to change the world, one meal at a time.

Jeanny Yao and Miranda Wang

In 2011 high school juniors Miranda Wang and Jeanny Yao wanted to solve an environmental problem after taking a field trip with their environmental club to a waste transfer station in Vancouver, British Columbia. It was there they saw firsthand how much plastic ended up in the garbage instead of being recycled. They put their heads together to solve this problem, and in 2015 created a company called Novoloop located in Menlo Park, California (near Google headquarters).

Their company gives plastic trash a new life! Novoloop takes trash that normally would take hundreds of years to break down in nature and shrinks it down in less than 6 hours. They transform that material into high-performance materials used in shoes, cars, homes, and more. Go to www.novoloop.com, or look up @jeannyYao and @mirandaywwang on Twitter.

Follow Jasmine Crowe and Goodr Online:

Website: www.feedingamerica.org and www.goodr.co

Instagram: @jasminecrowe, @feedingamerica, and @goodrco

Twitter: @jasminecrowe, @FeedingAmerica, and @TheGoodrCo

Facebook: Feeding America and GoodrCo

Part IV: Education

Sandra Oh Lin: KiwiCo

Sandra was a young girl when her parents decided to open a kiosk business at the mall. They sold troll dolls, the ones with the wild, colorful hair on top of their heads. Sandra's first responsibility was to name the business, and she decided on Wonderland. Sandra and her sister worked the Wonderland kiosk on weekends and evenings. They also separated their excess inventory and sold it at local flea markets for additional income. It was there that young Sandra learned how to display merchandise, price her products, and sell to customers—skills that would ultimately go on to make a huge impact on her life.

Sandra Oh Lin was born in Korea. When she was a baby, her parents immigrated to the United States and moved to North Carolina, where her father had been accepted into graduate school at the University of North Carolina. Her family moved again when Sandra was a toddler, this time to Fairfield, Ohio, where her father took a new job and Sandra's younger sister joined the family.

Growing up, Sandra's mother held various jobs, but first and foremost, she was a mom. In fact, Sandra's fondest memories of her childhood involve her mother, who was a very creative, hands-on, and resourceful person. "Every year my mother would hand-make Halloween costumes for my sister and me. One year we went as a pear and banana, but this was not just any pear and banana. These were beautiful, handcrafted costumes from fabric materials," Sandra recalls.

As a child, Sandra was always busy and staying active. She loved school, especially math and science, and had a natural passion for experimenting and searching for answers to the unknown. When she wasn't in school, Sandra played sports. She tore up the field in soccer, and enjoyed tennis, swimming, and basketball. Sandra also had a black belt in Tae Kwon Do!

During her downtime, Sandra enjoyed creating things with the help of her mother. Sandra's mother was a person who, in her daughters' eyes, could do anything, make anything and helped bring their visions to light. Sometimes they drove to McDonald's for a Happy Meal. Back then, McDonald's Happy Meals came with hamburgers that were placed in Styrofoam containers, which kept the burger toasty warm. Sandra collected the containers and turned them into crafty handbags. Her mother believed that just about anything could be reused and repurposed to become something new and fun.

Just like most children, Sandra dreamed about what she wanted to be when she grew up. As a young girl, she envisioned herself as a television anchor, a person who was knowledgeable about a wide range of global topics and could deliver that information to her audience in a comprehendible manner. But by the time Sandra entered high school, her dreams of television had vanished, and she had become passionate about science, considering either a career in medicine or engineering. Sandra attended Case Western Reserve University in Cleveland, Ohio. She played on the varsity soccer team and majored in chemical engineering, while minoring in economics and biology.

Sandra's First Jobs

Sandra's first job out of school was at Procter & Gamble, the company that makes Bounty, Pampers, Tide, and Crest. Her time there was invaluable, and Sandra learned how to conduct market research, gather information about what people wanted, and create new products to meet those needs. She also learned what makes a strong brand and the best ways to market and sell to large numbers of customers.

Two years later, Sandra's husband took a job on the East Coast and she got her master of business administration from Harvard University. But after she graduated from Harvard, it was Sandra's turn to steer the career ship. She moved the family out West and took a job at PayPal, then eBay. By 2010 Sandra was running eBay's $2 billion fashion business, plus she was the mom of two young children—a girl, age five, and a boy, age three.

Working full time and being a mom of two young children was hard and hectic, but Sandra found ways to keep her children busy with creative projects that kept them off the screens: "I created hands-on projects for them to exercise their creativity. Part of it was the engineer in me, who wanted to encourage my kids to have fun with hands-on, open-ended projects. Another part was probably nostalgia; I had so many fond memories doing cool projects with my mom, who was a maker herself."

Sandra created elaborate arts and crafts projects and science experiments. It was fun and rewarding to watch her children engage with such interest. These projects turned her kids into *producers*—someone who makes something—rather than *consumers*—someone who just uses something.

One day, Sandra invited some of her mom friends over and gave them a few of her handmade crafts to do. Everyone was amazed! One of the parents turned to Sandra and insisted, "You should start a business doing this." While Sandra was flattered, the business person inside her brain questioned the idea of a kids craft business. She asked herself, *Is making art and science projects for kids a viable business? Did other parents have the same problem I do? Would kids in other parts of the country enjoy the same type of projects children enjoy in California? What about kids who come from different backgrounds or demographics? How much would parents pay for it? What age group would enjoy it?* Millions of questions swirled in Sandra's brain, but she knew what she had to do: market research!

Ellen Eliza Fitz, Inventor of the Modern Globe

Ellen Fitz was working as a governess, which is like a nanny, in New Brunswick, Canada, when she invented the modern globe. It stood 12 inches high and had a special mounting system that showed the path of the sun and how daylight and nighttime show differently on different parts of the world. Her invention received a patent in 1875. Ellen Fitz was the first woman ever to design or manufacture a world globe, yet there is little information about the inventor and no photograph of her has ever been found.

The Idea

In early 2011 Sandra invited some friends, as well as friends of friends, into her living room and asked them dozens of questions. She also created a wide range of sample products and invited kids from the area to test them out in her garage. What she learned was fascinating. One, most parents were very busy but also well intentioned, meaning that they wanted only the best for their children. Two, kids did want to continually learn, make, and experiment with new things. And three, both parents and kids dreamed of a wonderful future for the child. If there was a way to combine all of this and make it fun, Sandra knew she was on to something.

Now she needed a name for the company. Sandra, once more, looked to her children for inspiration:

I was brainstorming, and in my house one of the stuffed animals that caught my eye was a stuffed kiwi bird from New Zealand. We loved New Zealand and how much that country is about nature and discovery and exploration. We thought it was a great tie-in with what we were trying to do with the company.

Sandra also liked how the Kiwi bird is curious, friendly, and a good companion, many of the qualities she hoped her company to be.

In October 2011 Sandra was ready to launch KiwiCo. The first product was called Kiwi Crate and provided kids (ages three to six) with ways to explore colors. There were three parts to the first Kiwi Crate. The first project let kids spin different colors together, and they could see for themselves what happened. For example, when red paint spun with yellow paint, it created orange paint. The second project was a stained-glass project. It included different tissue paper colors with various finishes. Children could create their own "stained glass" art by layering the tissue paper over each other. The third project included bleeding tissue paper that turned a plain old canvas bag into a work of art using nothing more than water and a dropper. Each craft brought an element of science and magic to help bring colors to life.

Elizabeth Magie Phillips, Inventor of Monopoly

Elizabeth Phillips was an independent woman who in 1903 invented a real estate game to portray the ins and outs of real estate, and why having a land monopoly is a bad thing. Just think how you feel when your sibling gets all the properties! She called it the Landlord's Game and patented it in 1904. "It is a practical demonstration of the present system of land-grabbing with all its usual outcomes and consequences," Elizabeth (who was called Lizzie by her friends) once wrote in a magazine. "It might well have been called the 'Game of Life,' as it contains all the elements of success and failure in the real world, and the object is the same as the human race in general seem to have, i.e., the accumulation of wealth."

Over the next two decades, the game became quite popular, and some players began to tweak the rules. In 1934, an unemployed man named Charles Darrow took the Landlord's Game along with a friend's version of the rules and printed it on cardboard. He started selling it as the Monopoly Game. One year later, Charles Darrow sold his "stolen" version to Parker Brothers. While the game started to take off, Parker Brothers bought up the rights to all board games similar to Monopoly, including Lizzie's. They paid her just $500. Monopoly eventually became the bestselling board game in America and has earned tens of millions of dollars.

Growing It

Sandra made sure that after each crate went out she followed up with a survey. Did the child enjoy the project? Why or why not? Was it easy to understand? Was it enjoyable? Were the parents satisfied? The data she collected helped make the next project even better.

Sandra started to notice as time went on that there might be an opportunity to create Kiwi kits for kids of different ages. In 2014 KiwiCo launched three new lines—Koala Crate, Kiwi Crate, and Doodle Crate—hoping one might work. Not only did they all work, but also, they all sold out! And because KiwiCo was developed as a subscription service, it meant that the customers automatically came back month after month. From that day, sales took off. In 2016 KiwiCo turned profitable.

Two of the most important "secrets" behind KiwiCo's success are the people who design the crates and those who test them out. Each crate is developed by a team of individuals with different backgrounds. There are mechanical engineers, artists, educators, designers, and even a NASA rocket scientist. Together, they put in 1,000 hours to make sure each crate has four things. First, all the contents in a KiwiCo box must be lightweight. This keeps the shipping costs low. Second, the crate must be visually appealing to kids. That means when a child opens up the box, the contents must look fun, exciting, and interesting. Third, each crate must be high quality and safe so parents are satisfied and no one gets injured. And finally, each crate must be easy to make, but challenging enough not to be considered boring or a waste of time. Needless to say, developing each month's crate is not an easy task!

In 2021 KiwiCo offered eight different crates: **Panda Crates** (ages 0–24 months), which include themes around play. **Koala Crates** (ages 2–4 years) might include something like a wooden fishing pole with felt fish and turtles. The child can practice catching the fish by color or size. **Kiwi Crate** (ages 5–8) is the signature crate and might include a make-it-yourself rocket or kite. **Atlas Crate** (ages 9–11) centers around different geographical locations and cultures; projects might include making a spinning globe or your own koinobori fluttering carp wind sock. **Doodle Crates** (age 9–16+) target older children with a passion for art. Projects might include making a felt succulent garden or handmade soap. **Tinker Crates** (ages 9–16+) focus on STEM (science, technology, engineering, and mathematics) and innovation. Kids might create a walking robot or a functioning trebuchet that launches a ping-pong ball up to 10 feet. **Maker Crates** (ages 14–104) are art projects for older "kids" who could create a macramé key chain or a traditional, mosaiclike art form called terrazzo. And finally, **Eureka Crates** (ages 14–104) focus on STEM projects for older "kids" and include things like pulleys and springs, electric motors and torque, or entail building real musical instruments.

Demand and sales steadily grew over the years. And then the COVID-19 pandemic hit in early 2020. For the first time ever, parents and kids suddenly found them themselves working and doing school from the same place—home! Parents desperately sought out a solution to keep their kids creative and engaged, and they wanted something that differed from the screen time they were getting through school, video games, and their phones. KiwiCo turned out to be the perfect solution. Sales went through the roof. "We ship out over 20 million crates now," Sandra explained. "If you look at the first ten million crates, we hit that mark in January 2019 (eight years after the company launched). Over the next 18 months, we shipped out the next ten million crates."

Sandra Oh Lin and KiwiCo Today

While KiwiCo brings STEM to children all over the world, Sandra says that one of the best parts of building this company was having her now three children by her side, inspiring her every step of the way: "I feel lucky that they've been a part of it." Sandra's children appear in videos and on the website and, more important, test Kiwi kits all the time.

Being grateful is also an aspect that makes Sandra such a humble and effective entrepreneur and leader. She practices gratitude daily, explaining, "I recognize that I'm incredibly fortunate. There are people and circumstances that have allowed me to do what I do, and, for that, I'm grateful." And when things do get hectic, Sandra finds herself back on the soccer field. "Although I'm now more of a soccer mom than a soccer player, I love playing when I can. I've played for years, and it always makes me happy to be on the field with a ball. It's my Zen place."

Sandra is a fearless and world-changing entrepreneur who never envisioned herself as one until it happened. But like most things, she's grateful to have founded KiwiCo and to bring STEM, art, and innovation to kids around the world. Her STEM tip for parents? "Give kids permission to explore—bang on different size pots, take apart an old clock, toast a marshmallow, question and observe."

Follow Sandra Oh Lin and KiwiCo Online:

Website: www.kiwico.com

Instagram: @kiwico_inc

Twitter: @sandraohlin and @kiwico_inc

Facebook: KiwiCo

Reshma Saujani: Girls Who Code

It was another long day planned during Reshma's campaign for Congress. She would be visiting several New York City classrooms to meet the teachers, see the classrooms, and watch the students hard at work. The principal welcomed Reshma to the first of many school visits, and escorted her down the hall toward their computer classroom, explaining how the students were learning about robotics, computers, technology, and coding. Understanding how important technology was to a good education and a promising future, they both agreed that the world's next great tech innovators were right there in the classroom. The principal opened the door for Reshma, and as she stepped in, she smiled at the children and looked at their young faces. However, one question popped into Reshma's head: *Where are the girls?*

Reshma Saujani was born into the safest environment her parents could create. In 1973 her parents, Meena and Mukund, had fled Uganda as political refugees. At the time, the country was led by a dangerous dictator, who had given all people from India 90 days to leave Uganda—or they would be shot. With no money, Reshma's parents risked their lives and escaped to the United States, settling in a western suburb of Chicago, Illinois, called Schaumburg. And while there were only a handful of Brown people in their neighborhood, they did their best to fit in.

Reshma's parents changed their names from Meena to Mina, and Mukund to Mike. Both Mina and Mike had worked as engineers in Uganda, but found different jobs in America. Mina took a job as a cosmetics salesperson, and Mike worked as a machinist in a factory. They did everything they could to fit into their new life in America. Mike worked on dropping his Indian accent by attending weekly meetings with the local Toastmasters group. As a family they ate American fast food, went to the movies, and worked hard at school and their jobs. Mike and Mina's goal was to raise a family in a safe community where their two daughters, Reshma and Keshma, could get a good education and become doctors, lawyers, or engineers. Their message to their children was to work hard, keep quiet, live nonviolently, and not rock the boat. But Reshma was never satisfied with that plan.

When Reshma was a little girl, her father read her stories from *Reader's Digest* each night. These stories featured great American heroes like Martin Luther King Jr. and Eleanor Roosevelt. A fire started to brew inside young Reshma. She wanted to give back to the country that saved her parents. She wanted to make a difference like the heroes portrayed in the stories her father read to her. And she started to struggle with the fact that she didn't want to follow her parents' rules of keeping quiet. Instead, Reshma wanted to speak up. She wanted to give back. She wanted to help people. And, against her parents' wishes, she wanted to rock the boat!

But being different from everyone else at her school was not always easy for Reshma. She was bullied and teased throughout her childhood. Her family's house was often vandalized with eggs smashed against windows or toilet paper thrown in the trees. One time, someone spray-painted "dot head go home" on their house. Mean girls called Reshma a "hajji" to her face, an insult against people of Middle Eastern and Indian descent. They threatened her with violence.

Finally, one day in eighth grade, Reshma decided to fight back. After school, Reshma agreed to meet some of the mean girls for a fight and came armed with a tennis racket and can of shaving cream. Unfortunately, she found not just one or two girls ready to fight but what appeared to be half the school. The mob attacked Reshma on the spot—she was knocked out cold. And when she woke, she dragged herself home, bloody and beat up. Reshma showed up a few days later for her eighth-grade graduation, boldly wearing a pretty lace dress, bright pink lipstick, and an enormous black and blue eye, a reminder to all who had given it to her that nothing would ever bring her down.

At age 13, Reshma led her first march in school. When she got to high school, she started the first diversity group. Reshma dreamed that she would become a lawyer one day, a respectable job that her parents approved of. A lawyer, she decided, was a job that could make right from wrong. Reshma worked hard in school and started on a path to that goal. She earned good grades and attended the University of Illinois at Urbana-Champaign, then Harvard's Kennedy School of Government for graduate school.

Reshma knew she needed to attend law school to become a lawyer and set her sights on the prestigious Yale Law School, a school she believed would help make her dreams come true. So, Reshma applied to Yale Law School . . . but she was rejected. She decided one rejection would not stand in her way of the law degree that she believed was her ticket to success, so she applied again. . . . and was rejected again. Reshma applied a third time to Yale Law School . . . and was rejected for a third time. But just like she had bravely faced those mean girls in eighth grade, Reshma knew this hurdle would not bring her down. So she applied a fourth time and finally, Reshma was accepted into Yale Law School!

Reshma's First Jobs

By the time she was 33 years old, Reshma was living in New York City, and had the degree in government and the law degree she had always dreamed of. But also, she had accumulated $300,000 of school debt. Reshma took a job in the corporate world and worked long, grueling hours. It was everything she and her parents had hoped for, and she was making good money, but Reshma wasn't happy. *Is this it? Is this the rest of my life?* Reshma asked herself again and again while grinding away late at night, still at work.

Reshma felt empty. She felt alone. One day, she picked up the phone and called her best friend, then burst into tears. Her best friend listened, then said two words: "Just quit." It had never occurred to Reshma that she could "just quit" a job she didn't like.

A few days later, Reshma quit her job and set out on a new plan: politics. Reshma wanted to lead her community and help people, and she thought the answer lay in politics. In 2010 Reshma decided to run for office, making her the first South Asian American woman to run for Congress. The campaign would be tough. She was up against an incumbent, a woman who had held the office for 18 years. But from day one, Reshma's campaign took off. She raised over $1 million for her campaign. She hit the streets, meeting with people, listening to their concerns, and expressing her viewpoints and positions on issues. She was featured on the cover of local and national newspapers. She was endorsed by the *New York Daily News*. And CNBC called it one of the hottest races in the country.

As part of her campaign run, Reshma visited dozens of schools throughout New York City to see what went on in the classrooms. Reshma walked into traditional classrooms as well as computer rooms, but at every school she looked around the technology classrooms and wondered, *Where are the girls?*

The classrooms were filled with dozens of boys, but barely a girl could be found. This discovery troubled Reshma. It sat with her for days, weeks, months. And it would eventually lead to something huge.

Great Women in Coding

Ada Lovelace, First Computer Programmer

Ada Lovelace (1815–1852) was an English mathematician best known for working on Charles Babbage's general-purpose computer. In 1843 Ada was only 27 years old and published step-by-step operating instructions on how to "program" this analytical engine, making it the world's first computer program. Ada was also the first person to figure out that computers can do things beyond just calculation. The second Tuesday of October is now known as Ava Lovelace Day.

Grace Hopper, Computer Scientist and Navy Admiral

Grace Hopper (1906–1992) was an American computer scientist as well as a rear admiral for the US Navy. Grace developed the theory of machine-independent programming languages and her FLOW-MATIC programming language led to the creation of COBOL—a programming language that is use today.

Sister Mary Kenneth Keller, Computer Science Pioneer

Sister Mary Kenneth Keller (1913–1985) was a nun and pioneer in computer science. She became the first American woman to receive a PhD in computer science and helped developed the computer programming language BASIC.

The ENIAC Six Programmers

This incredible group of women programmed the first electronic computer in 1945 without the help of programming tools or language. Their names are Kathleen McNulty Mauchly Antonelli, Jean Jennings Bartik, Frances Snyder Holder, Marlyn Wescoff Meltzer, Frances Bilas Spence, and Ruth Lichterman Teitelbaum.

The Idea

Reshma lost the race for Congress. And despite all the hype around her campaign, she lost badly—with only 19 percent of the vote. Reshma spent the days following the election with a wide range of emotions. She was sad, angry, defeated, frustrated, and humiliated. But despite this emotional roller coaster, she couldn't shake that one question from her mind: *Where were the girls in those computer classrooms?*

In India, where her parents were originally from, 50 percent of engineers and coders were women. The same was true for countries like Italy, China, and Russia. So why were the numbers so different in the United States? Reshma did some research and made several eye-opening discoveries. She discovered that in the 1970s and 1980s women filled college computer science classrooms in the United States and made up half of Apple's first computer programming team. But by 2013 only 18 percent of college computer classes were women. Again, Reshma wondered . . . where *did* all the girls go?

Reshma's research uncovered more troubling trends, beginning with the early marketing campaigns run by computer companies like Apple and IBM. When the first personal computers were launched in the 1980s, they marketed their products to adults and boys. Not girls. Computers were advertised as the next great toy for boys. Reshma read story after story of how the founders of successful technology companies such as Google, Facebook, and Twitter had one thing in common—their parents had purchased them a computer when they were in middle school or junior high. Reshma uncovered more troubling themes from movies in the 1980s and '90s in popular films such as *Weird Science, War Games,* and *Ferris Bueller's Day Off.* Here the smart, clever, or nerdy boys were all computer geniuses. A girl was never was the computer genius. Reshma looked for books that taught girls how to code, but none existed. She realized she had to do something.

In 2012 Reshma launched a nonprofit organization called Girls Who Code. She kept the name simple and the mission bold: teach girls how to code. Her goal was to reverse the downward trend in computer science and keep girls interested in STEM through their junior high and high school years. Within her lifetime, Reshma was certain Girls Who Code would help equalize the number of computer-related jobs between men and women. Girls Who Code would prepare hundreds of thousands of girls for the 1.4 million jobs in computer-related fields.

Nonprofit: A nonprofit organization is run similarly to a for-profit organization in that managers operate the business for success and try to earn a profit. But nonprofit organizations differ in that their purpose is to further a social cause and provide a public benefit. A nonprofit's profit is used only for the advancement of the organization, not the benefit of anything else.

Twenty girls from New York City were brought together for a seven-week "experiment." They came from different backgrounds that ranged from prestigious private schools to underprivileged neighborhoods. None of the 20 girls had a computer science background. Reshma borrowed a conference room from a friend's company and thanked him with a free pizza lunch.

Over the course of the seven weeks, the girls came together as a powerful group of thinkers, teammates, and leaders. "By the end of the summer, I saw something magical," Reshma recalled. "I saw girls who began as strangers call each other sisters. I saw girls who thought coding was only for boys, gain new role models that looked like them. And I saw girls who never thought they'd be interested in coding build apps and websites solving issues that tugged at their heartstrings."

As the Girls Who Code classes expanded to new cities, the coding instructors began noticing a common trend among many of the girls. In the beginning of the course, many of the girls were afraid to show their coding programs unless they were perfect. The girls were afraid to show their mistakes. They were afraid to ask for help. If it wasn't perfect, they weren't proud. Sometimes the girls preferred to stare at a blank screen rather than work away at a screen filled with errors—errors they could learn and grow from. This observation bothered Reshma. She realized that maybe a bigger problem existed behind why girls weren't coding. Maybe the girls weren't being raised to be risk-takers or to be comfortable with mistakes. Perhaps this was also an important message to communicate.

Growing It

Reshma began speaking all over the country about Girls Who Code, about her mission to close the gender gap in technology, and, most important, about teaching girls to be "Brave, Not Perfect," which has become her motto. Then something incredible started to happen. More and more girls started signing up for Girls Who Code classes.

They signed up in after-school programs in elementary schools, middle schools, junior high schools, and high schools. They signed up by the tens of thousands! Girls Who Code offered a seven-week Summer Immersion Program, a two-week specialized Campus Program, after-school clubs, and even a book series called Girls Who Code. Girls Who Code opened classes in every state. They expanded to India, Canada, England, and Scotland. By 2016, 30,000 girls were enrolled. By 2018, 50,000 girls were enrolled. And by 2021, 411,000 girls were enrolled!

Clubs were led by teachers, computer scientists, librarians, and parents—and the girls came from everywhere. The Girls Who Code website now states: "The demographic of Girls Who Code is the demographic of our nation. From Clubs in rural Oklahoma, to homeless shelters in Massachusetts, to the country's most prestigious private schools—girls everywhere are united by their passion to use technology to solve problems in their day-to-day lives and make a positive impact on the world."

Reshma Saujani and Girls Who Code Today

In February 2021 Reshma stepped down as the CEO (Chief Executive Officer) of Girls Who Code and handed the reins over to Dr. Tarika Barrett. Reshma remains the chairman of the board and continues to speak all over the world about her mission to close the gender gap in technology by teaching girls to code. "I want to give girls the opportunity to be the next Mark Zuckerberg," Reshma stated. "I won't be satisfied until I get every company in America to sign up and until I reach every girl in America."

What's Reshma most proud of? Teaching girls to take risks. Teaching girls to invite failure into their lives. And, ultimately, teaching girls to be brave, not perfect.

Follow Reshma Saujani and Girls Who Code Online:

Website: https://girlswhocode.com/

Instagram: @reshmasaujani and @girlswhocode

Twitter: @reshmasaujani and @GirlsWhoCode

Facebook: Girls Who Code

12

Cindy Mi: VIPKid

It was lunchtime and, as usual, Cindy Mi had skipped it. Instead, she pocketed her lunch money and opened the magazine she had recently purchased with her previous week's savings, focusing intensely on the words. The magazine was expensive because it was written in English and Cindy—who only spoke Chinese at the time—was determined to learn English. By the time she was 15, Cindy had become so proficient that she was tutoring other kids at her school. And that was just the beginning of her quest to teach the world how to speak English.

Cindy Mi grew up in China. When she was 14 years old, her family moved from Hebei to Harbin, a large city in the country's Heilongjiang Province. It took some time to move, and when her family finally settled into a new home near a new school, six months had passed. Cindy was behind in most of her classes, especially math. Her new classroom was overcrowded with 60 students, and Cindy's teacher didn't have time to help her catch up. In fact, the teacher not only didn't help her, Cindy remembered, "She hated me! She thought I was the dumbest person in the world." Every day, Cindy asked for help in class, but every day, her teacher ignored her pleas. Eventually, Cindy gave up. She became discouraged and lost confidence in herself. She even started to hide science-fiction magazines in her math notebooks and read them during class instead of trying to learn, which seemed hopeless. One day, the teacher found her magazines, ripped them up, and threw them in Cindy's face! Frustrated and angry, the teacher told Cindy to leave immediately and never return! Cindy recalled, "I left the classroom like a hero, but I had to return to school the next day, begging for her to take me back. I lost all my confidence in learning."

Cindy's First Jobs

At age 17 Cindy dropped out of school. She was proficient in English and was tutoring other students how to speak English. And instead of continuing with her own education in a traditional classroom, she founded an English tutoring company with her uncle called ABC English.

Tutoring was a big business in China. Chinese parents took after-school learning very seriously and on average spent 15 percent of their annual income on after-school tutoring, a significant difference to the 2 percent of annual income that US parents spent on their children's after-school tutoring. Cindy's parents supported their daughter's decision to quit school and become an entrepreneur, but boldly said, "Make the decision and don't come back in tears." It was that tough-love attitude that taught Cindy at an early age she had freedom to make independent choices about her life, but also was responsible for them.

At ABC English, Cindy became the "Chief of Errands." Her responsibilities included purchasing the tutoring books, running sales, interviewing teachers, driving teachers to and from the classroom (often for miles!), grading homework, meeting students, talking to parents, and preparing the next day's curriculum. She worked very late into the evening, often until 2:00 AM each night. But her hard work paid off, and ABC English became a successful company with $30 million in sales annually.

Chinese Education: English education is very important in China, so much so that the Organization for Economic Cooperation and Development wrote that the "Chinese government saw education as the primary tool for national development." After the Chinese government declared speaking English as one of the most important aspects of national competitiveness, tutoring businesses popped up all over the country. By 2014, more than 50,000 private language schools were operating throughout China. The biggest English tutoring company in China is New Oriental Education & Technology Group, which was founded by a professor named Yu Minhong in 1993. These in-person classes are often very expensive and don't reach children in rural areas.

The Idea

While at ABC English, Cindy spent a lot of time with the students, parents, and teachers. "I got the privilege to understand what every parent and child wants," she explained. And three things became very clear. One, each child learns very differently and can excel academically if paired with the correct teacher. Thinking back to her math class at age 14, Cindy knew that yelling, ignoring, and being mean to a child does not work. On the other hand, she had seen first-hand how a child can shine with one-on-one encouragement and individual attention. Two, Cindy started to understand that there were very few good English teachers living in China. Only 27,000 English native teachers lived in China at the time, and they were in high demand. The next-best English teachers available were young adults with little teaching experience and minimal English experience. Finally, parents valued opportunities that provided a great education for their child as well as an easy way to give it to them. Lugging children to crowded tutoring classes on the weekends or after school was often frustrating for parents, and they longed for an easier solution.

Armed with that knowledge, Cindy had an idea. She wanted to create an online one-on-one English tutoring solution. Her company would connect Chinese children who wanted a high-quality English tutoring program with teachers from North America, where English was the native language and great teachers were abundant. One teacher would be paired with one student so that the child could receive personal attention. Everything would take place online and with the time difference between China and North America, teachers could log on very early in the morning before going to work (between 4:00 AM and 7:00 AM), which was equivalent to after school for Chinese children.

Cindy called her business idea VIPKid and launched it in October 2013. But when she approached investors, they didn't understand her vision: "The first 18 months were very challenging. Nobody bought the idea from either side of the marketplace. They thought it was too challenging to teach. Investors thought it was a dumb idea." Cindy didn't give up. She patiently continued to explain her idea to students, parents, teachers, and investors.

Cindy knew that the key to her success was her teacher network. She brought on 10 qualified teachers from the United States who believed in her idea and needed the extra income. Next, she needed students in China. But no one signed up!

Cindy finally had 10 students who were willing to try out VIPKid, most of them were children of people she knew. And when paired with the right teacher, something beautiful happened. These two strangers came together as teammates in a quest to learn English. In addition, the child and teacher who were from opposite sides of the earth connected with each other, sharing their culture and way of life. It was magical! Cindy remembered one seven-year-old girl looking at a screen and saying, "Teacher, come back, where are you?"

As word started to spread, teachers began referring other teachers and applications flowed in. But VIPKid wouldn't accept just any teacher. They had to have several important qualities:

Teachers must love children.

Teachers must be very patient with the children.

Teachers must want to help each child learn and grow.

Teachers must have a bachelor's degree in education.

Teachers must know how to communicate without speaking a common language with the child.

Cindy trained teachers to communicate online using nonverbal positive communication, reinforcement, hand gestures, and tone. Then, as more children signed up, Cindy sought ways to reach children in rural areas, not just in the populous cities. She knew that 56 percent of children in rural areas of China don't receive a good education, and she was determined to change that. VIPKid could give everyone a chance at a better education and a better life.

Growing It

Word spread quickly among parents, and VIPKid started to grow. Cindy's idea for a high-quality education program in the cloud was becoming a reality:

> It's a future, cloud-based school, where all the students, from everywhere, can learn from all the teachers. . . . The benefits for the students are very tremendous, because then they can have a teacher, out of the 60,000 teachers, that is the most appropriate for the child, that can really create this curiosity for learning, and we match it with

technology, so students can get the best teacher, due to their personality preferences, or the learning style, or the other parents' comment, based on the teacher, and then they pay way less.

As more students signed up, teacher applications poured in from all 50 states. Instructors loved working with VIPKid for many reasons. It fit their schedule well, it provided extra income, and they were making a difference in children's lives. Soon, VIPKid teachers started creating their own events and giving each other tips on how to best teach English to Chinese-speaking children.

With the extra income they had earned from VIPKid tutoring, Cindy heard stories of how teachers could finally afford a new car or pay for their child's college education or take a vacation or put a mortgage down on their house. They also fell in love with the children in China. As Cindy explained:

So, we were in this teacher conference, it's called Journey, teachers initiate it, and they organized a conference themselves . . . and the former First Lady Laura Bush joined the conference, and then 400 teachers got together, everyone just shared their passion about teaching children in China, and teachers tell me, they say, "Oh, my students—Jenny, she is my other daughter, in China," and some teachers even share their story of their visiting China on their own expense, and then they say, "I walk around my neighborhood, and tell my neighbors, and I say, 'Chinese people are amazing, the kids are so smart, the parents really respect me.'" You know, one time, one of our teachers had her birthday, and then, on the other side of the screen, it's the whole family, not just the kid, but candles—like, grandparents, parents, and then they almost bow to the teachers, because we respect the teachers so much in China, and they really respect and appreciate everything the teacher has done for them.

The Pack Horse Librarians

The Pack Horse Library initiative was created during the Great Depression to encourage learning and literacy in the United States' most hard-hit areas. As part of this effort, librarians—who were mostly women—were sent out on horseback to deliver library books to people deep in the Appalachian Mountains. The librarians rode through rain, wind, sleet, and mud delivering books, magazines, and newspapers to those who could not travel. Sometimes the land was so rugged that the librarians had to get off the horse and travel by foot. These librarians were true literary heroes.

Cindy Mi and VIPKid Today

VIPKid is now one of the largest China-based online English tutoring platforms, with 70,000 teachers in the United States and Canada, and 600,000 students online. Most kids have short 15- to 20-minute English lessons each day, which works better than one long lesson once a week. Cindy has helped children learn English in the best way possible. And she has helped children and teachers connect from opposite sides of the globe.

Ultimately, Cindy's goal with VIPKid is to create more than just an English tutoring company. She wants to create a generation of global citizens—children who could learn about the rest of the world through culture, language, and interaction. "What if you had students gathering around the pyramids virtually to learn everything about them?" Cindy wondered. "What if you had a classroom of students, each from a different country, talking to each other in a global channel? In my beautiful future dreams, I see children learning from one another."

Follow Cindy Mi and VIPKid Online:

Website: www.vipkid.com

Instagram: @thevipkidlife

Twitter: @Wenjuan_Mi and @TheVIPKIDLife

Facebook: VIPKid

Part V: Clothing and Fashion

Heidi Zak: ThirdLove

When Heidi Zak was 11 years old, it was time for that often-dreaded reality in life—buying her first bra. She wasn't entirely sure she needed a bra yet, but most of her friends had them, so she asked her mom if they could go bra shopping. Heidi's mom decided they would go together with her grandmother.

"It was terrible!" Heidi recalls. "My mom decided to take me when we were visiting my grandma in Pittsburgh, and they brought me to a JCPenney store. We walked into the massive store with a wall full of training bras. They called the sales associate over and they were all talking really loudly—talking about me like I wasn't even there!" Heidi's face turned red, and she wanted to hide. "I was so embarrassed and hated every minute of it." Little did she know at the time that life would take her on a path to solve this problem not only for girls and teenagers but also for women of all ages.

Heidi grew up in Youngstown, New York, along the Niagara River. Located just minutes from the incredible Niagara Falls, her town of only 3,000 people overlooked Lake Ontario—and residents could see Toronto, Canada, on the other side of the water. The only child in her family, Heidi found many ways to keep busy as a young girl. At age seven, she started training competitively in gymnastics. By the time she was nine years old, she was putting in 20 hours a week at the gym, working hard to become an elite athlete. Heidi was also always one of the top-performing students at her school year after year. "I just loved learning," Heidi remembers. "I loved school, I loved keeping busy. In fact, my father used to say the biggest punishment they could give me was to take things away from me and make me bored!"

When Heidi was in fifth grade, her teacher asked the kids in the class to think about what they wanted to be when they grow up, identify their idol, and write a report on that person and his or her job. Heidi chose Katie Couric, the coanchor of the *Today Show* from 1991 to 2006. She wrote a long report about how fascinating it was being a television anchor and how incredible Katie Couric was at her job. And while she got an A+ on the report, this story would be helpful later in her life, too.

As Heidi entered high school, two things became clear: she was more interested in making money than being on television as a news anchor, and she no longer wanted to compete in gymnastics. She kept up her good grades, and since much of the surrounding area was farmland, she took a job at age 14 working at a local farmers' market. There, her eyes widened to the opportunities of business.

Heidi explains:

I had my first job at 14 and made $4.25/hour. I worked at a farm market in my town that was open from spring to fall. It was called Tom Towers Farm Market. It was a really nice farm market and the farmer who ran it—even though he looked like a regular farmer with dirty overalls—had a very high attention to detail. Everything had to be perfect. He had old-fashioned cash registers from the 1800s to create an authentic and natural feel. He taught me what color products should be next to each other and which shouldn't. For example, instead of putting two red fruits beside each other, we would break them up with an eggplant or something. I learned how to sell, how to greet customers, how to push the freshest products. I learned all about the concept of customer service and merchandising.

It was also a great experience for building good work habits. Every morning for several summers, Heidi woke at 5:00 AM, arrived at her job at 6:00 AM, and began setting up the farmers' market for the day.

After high school, Heidi attended Duke University, where she majored in economics and taught gymnastics at the local YMCA. Her junior year, Heidi took a class called Markets and Management. It was the closest thing Duke offered to an entrepreneurship class at the time, and concluded with each student coming up with an idea, a business plan, and pitching it.

"It was awesome," Heidi says. "I partnered with a friend of mine and our idea was to create a women's apparel company for young women who needed suits. I knew that women who worked in banking or on Wall Street wanted something more stylish than what was out there for older women. It was sort of the Anne Taylor for young women."

But even then, Heidi didn't realize she wanted to be an entrepreneur: "Definitely not. If you would have asked me [then], I would've said, 'Not in a million years.' I think there are a few reasons for that. One is that when I was in school, entrepreneurship was not as mainstream of a concept as it is today. I probably wouldn't have even been able to name one female entrepreneur back then."

Heidi's First Jobs

Heidi's first jobs were quite traditional for someone with her educational background and interest. She worked in investment banking at Bank of America and as a consultant for McKinsey. She attended business school at MIT where she met a man named Dave Spector. (Dave would eventually become her husband.) After business school, Heidi took a job at the clothing store Aéropostale in New York City. It was there that she learned all about the world of fashion, including the steps of designing a product, selling it, and branding it.

In 2010 Heidi was offered a job at Google in the marketing department. She and David decided to pick up and move out to

Mountain View, California, not knowing that a world of entrepreneurship lay ahead of them. Heidi was fascinated by the start-up energy in the air. It seemed that everyone she met was a founder who was passionate and excited about their ideas. It made Heidi's mind swirl. . . . Could she do this as well? "When I moved to San Francisco and I started meeting people who were founding their own businesses, I had an epiphany: 'If all these people can build businesses and impact the world in a really meaningful way, why can't I?'"

One day, Heidi and Dave attended a company's launch party. The founders were friends of Dave's and their business was called Zimride. Approximately 20 people, mostly engineers and coders, attended the party. Heidi walked around that evening asking them what Zimride was. When she heard it was an app that would connect people who needed a ride with people willing to drive them in their own car, Heidi cringed. She thought it was a terrible idea! In fact, she left the party thinking if Zimride could be a company, she could certainly think of something better than that. (Zimride would later become Lyft, which is now a multibillion-dollar company!)

The Idea

Shortly thereafter, Heidi was running low on bras and knew it was time to go bra shopping. She reluctantly drove to the mall and located a Victoria's Secret store. But as Heidi walked into the bright pink store with loud music, strong perfume smells, and blinding lights, she winced. She hated shopping at Victoria's Secret. To manage the experience, she devised a plan. She would grab 20 bras in a size she thought was hers (34B), scoot to a dressing room, quickly try them on, purchase one or two, and leave as fast as possible.

As Heidi headed toward the dressing room, a saleswoman asked if she needed help. Heidi avoided eye contact and closed the dressing room door. Phew! Quickly, she pulled on each bra, chose the least offensive one (even though she didn't like it that much) and checked out as fast as possible. She explained, "I came out and I took the pink striped bag and stuffed it in my bag because I was embarrassed I'd been shopping there."

And then it hit her: "I was embarrassed that I was shopping for a bra that doesn't fit at a store that doesn't resonate with me." She thought other women probably felt the same way. She also wondered why she had to go to a mall to buy a bra when so many other clothing products could be purchased online. Perhaps there was a better way to shop for a better bra product and do it all online.

Heidi shared her idea for an online bra company with her now husband, Dave, explaining that it would provide women with the most comfortable, best-fitting bra in the world. Plus, they would educate women on how bras should fit, how they should care for it, and how to find the right size—all from the comfort of their own home: "In 2012, if you look at what had existed [for bra shopping] at that time, there were department stores, Victoria's Secret, and some big box stores. There certainly weren't online bra brands at the time. And that was the idea: better brand, better product, better online shopping experience for women."

Dave loved the idea. He was on board from day one.

But before Heidi jumped into launching a new company, she needed to do some research. Was her idea viable? She researched the size of the bra market, the competition in the bra industry, and how to create the product. She learned about different styles, the wide range of sizes, various fabrics, and how to care for bras. Next, she worked on a business plan. But since she was still working at Google, she didn't sleep much: "I would get home around 8:00 or 9:00 PM and then work on my business plan at night."

In 2012 Heidi felt confident that her idea had great potential. She would create an online bra company that would provide the most comfortable and stylish bras for women of all shapes and sizes. Heidi quit her job at Google and was ready to launch ThirdLove.

The name ThirdLove evolved after long consideration about what she wanted her bra company to represent, to look like, and how it would make others feel: "We didn't want to look like any other bra brand which mostly photographed skinny, generally white women with small boobs and generally did it in a really sexy way. So, we set out to build something radically different from scratch. . . . Back then there were barely any plus-size models." Heidi decided they would use models of women in all sizes and skin colors. Her brand name would represent strength and empowerment.

Now for the product. Thinking about bras, Heidi had always thought there were only two options: comfort or style. Comfortable bras were often not beautiful, while stylish bras were usually uncomfortable. She wanted her bra company to be that third option—it could be both. ThirdLove represented the third option. ThirdLove was the perfect name.

The more Heidi learned about bras, the more ideas she had. Bras have two measurements, the number, which is the band size in inches around the girl or women's rib cage to the bottom of her chest, and the cup size, which is the size of the actual breast. At the time, cup sizes came in AA (smallest), A, B, C, D, E, F, etc. But Heidi learned that 80 percent of women were wearing the wrong size bra. In fact, she soon learned that she, too, was wearing the wrong size bra. She also learned that, on average, most women have 10 bras in their top drawer but only wore one or two. The most common complaints about bras were that they didn't fit or were uncomfortable.

The Modern Bra

What we know as the modern bra was invented in 1913 by a 19-year-old Manhattan socialite named Mary Phelps, who later changed her name to Caresse Crosby. While Mary was getting dressed for a debutante ball, she did not like how the evening dress she had chosen revealed her corset underneath. A corset was very confining and restrictive undergarment that women used to wear under their clothes. It cinched a woman's waist as small as it would go and smashed her breasts together! Mary and her maid quickly pulled together some handkerchiefs and ribbon to create a new undergarment that was less restricting and allowed the plunging neckline of the dress to show her cleavage. Needless to say, Mary's invention stole the show, and she patented the "brassiere" soon thereafter.

How could Heidi fix these problems?

First, she questioned why cup sizes only came in full letter sizes like A, B, C. . . . Maybe part of the problem was that not all busts fit a full-size cup. She asked herself, *If shoes came in half sizes, why shouldn't bras?*

It took two years to get the company off the ground, and Heidi admits it was hard and full of mistakes. She and Dave used their savings to make the first prototypes and build their company.

Growing It

By 2014 Heidi was on her way to success. ThirdLove became the first company in the world to introduce bras in half sizes. And they didn't stop there. As they worked through the prototypes, she uncovered more problems with bras. For example, women and girls do not like tags in their bras. So, ThirdLove bras are completely tagless. Hooks and eye closure can be uncomfortable and scratchy. So, ThirdLove bras added comfy foam-padded hooks. Uncomfortable wires were replaced with flexible, nylon-coated, nickel-free material. Regular cups were replaced with soft, memory-foam padding. Each product was tested on employees and customers, and only those that fit well and preferred by as many women as possible were selected. Over time, ThirdLove gathered tens of thousands of women's measurements and used that data to improve the perfect fit.

As ThirdLove grew, they kept inclusivity at the forefront of their business: "We've built an inclusive brand by showing different body types, ethnicities, and ages in our campaigns. When we launched our extended sizes earlier this year, our photoshoot included real women of every single size and shape," Heidi said. "When we set out to film the commercial, we initially considered going the traditional route of using models, but we wanted to be real. And so, we decided to cast women that weren't models instead. We went onto the streets of Brooklyn and found real women who were willing to be featured in our campaign. . . . You would expect a lot of women to say no because they wouldn't want to be in their bras on TV, but a lot of women are like, 'I'm comfortable with my body—I confidently wear my bathing suit around—so what's the difference?'"

As the company grew, Heidi's savings ran out, and she had to raise money to continue to move the company in the right direction. It was then that she came across a new problem. Most of the investors she was pitching to were men who had never worn a bra. They didn't know that bras were uncomfortable or unflattering. They didn't know the embarrassment of buying a bra in a store. They didn't know what life with a bra was like! Could she convince men to invest in ThirdLove?

The Sports Bra

The sports bra was not invented until 1977, when three women at the University of Vermont's theater program came up with the idea. Their names were Lisa Lindahl, Hinda Miller, and Polly Smith. Lisa was a runner, and while she loved running, it was painful because of the lack of support around her breasts. According to the National Inventors Hall of Fame, Lisa "made a list of qualities an athletic bra should have, including stable straps, no chafing from seams or clasps, breathable fabric, and enough compression to prevent excessive movement." Lisa asked her friend Polly Smith, who was a costume designer, to create it. The first jog bra came together with two of Lisa's husband's jockstraps sewn together. Hinda Miller joined the team and helped grow the company into the first sports bra company for women.

At first, Heidi was devastated at what happened. Often, potential male investors would call a female employee into the meeting and ask her in front of everyone, "What do you think of these bras?" This was never a comfortable situation for anyone! So, Heidi learned to tweak her pitches. For men, she often talked more about financial data, while for female investors she talked about the real problem.

Before long, Heidi had many prominent investors, including Sara Blakely (Spanx), Anne Wojcicki (23andMe), and Heidi's childhood idol, *Today Show* anchor Katie Couric. In that first meeting with Katie, Heidi shared that she had written a fifth-grade report on the famous television anchor. Katie laughed, but more important, turned the meeting's focus back to Heidi and ThirdLove. It was then that Heidi realized Katie Couric was just as interested in Heidi as she had been with Katie when she was a little girl.

Heidi Zak and ThirdLove Today

Today, ThirdLove is the third-biggest online bra and underwear company in the world, with 80 different bra sizes and multiple styles. Their online Fit Finder quiz helps girls and women find the perfect bra in 10 questions. No more going into embarrassing stores. No more wearing the wrong size. And no more compromising comfort or style.

Since launching ThirdLove in 2012, Heidi Zak has also won many prestigious awards, including EY's Entrepreneur of the Year and Fast Company's Most Creative People. She is also doing everything she can to support female entrepreneurs of color with grants and mentoring. The company launched a program called TL Effect and explained, "If we can contribute to the success of more female founders of color, they will be able to hire others, and impact the world, and then mentor others over time. We see this as mutually beneficial—listening and learning from these founders' experiences and points of view can ultimately help affect change within our company and community."

Heidi's tip for young girls? You *can* have an amazing impact on the world. Focus on the things you love, the things you are naturally good at, and you'll find your way to work on those things. No one has it perfect, but be grateful for what is good in your life. If you have that determination, you can get through the tough times and persevere.

Bra Tips for Girls

There's no right or wrong age to start wearing bras, but Heidi's biggest tip is comfort! "A bra should feel good. It should feel so good, you stop thinking about your bra. If you're thinking about your bra, you either have the wrong size or the wrong style on."

How to put on a bra: There are a few tips for putting on a bra. First, start with the bra on the loosest hook. Over time, the elastic will stretch, and you will move to the middle hook, then the tightest hook. Adjust the shoulder straps so that the band is parallel across your back. You may have to adjust your shoulder straps up to one time per week. Heidi suggests leaning forward when putting on a bra so that the breasts fall into the cup, then swoop it up. Voilà!

How to wash a bra: Always clasp the hooks of a bra together and place it in a mesh bag with or without other bras. Wash bras on cold water and air-dry them. Never put it in a dryer, or the elastic will break down quickly.

Follow Heidi Zak and ThirdLove Online:

Website: www.thirdlove.com

Instagram: @Heidi and @ThirdLove

Twitter: @HeidiZaks and @ThirdLove

Facebook: ThirdLove

Jenn Hyman: Rent the Runway

Jenn Hyman and her business school friend Jenny Fleiss were in their rental car just blocks away from the office of famous clothing designer Diane von Furstenberg when Jenn's cell phone rang. "Hello?" she answered. "Hi, this is Diane von Furstenberg's office," a voice on the other line said. "Diane von Furstenberg doesn't want to see you after all. The meeting has been cancelled."

Jenn's mind quickly shifted into survival mode. She knew this meeting was their big break—she *had* to share her business idea with Diane von Furstenberg—an idea for *renting* designer clothes instead of buying them. Jenn made some static crackling noises with her mouth. *Crackle—whoosh—crackle—*"What? What?"*—crackle—crackle—crackle—*"You're breaking up. I can't hear you." Jenn fibbed, then quickly hung up the phone.

She looked at Jenny, her eyes wide with fierce determination, then pressed the gas pedal. They were *not* going to let this opportunity slip through their fingers. Moments later, Jenn and Jenny walked into Diane's office insisting they had no idea the meeting had been canceled and since they were there, they just needed a few minutes of Diane's time. Diane von Furstenberg agreed to meet with them.

Jennifer Hyman grew up in New Rochelle, New York, a suburb outside New York City. She was the oldest of four kids, three girls and a boy. After Jenn's youngest sister was born with severe autism, Jenn's mom quit her job in finance to stay home and raise their children. Jenn attended a small private Jewish school from kindergarten to eighth grade. She worked hard in school, played with her friends on the weekends, and was adored by her parents and grandparents. Early on, Jenn also realized she had a knack for business. Every year, her Jewish school sold Passover candy to raise money. "It's disgusting," Jenn later admitted of the Passover candy, because it didn't contain any dairy or flour. But the poor taste didn't stop Jenn. "I'd sell the hell out of it, more than anyone else. I'd go to untapped neighborhoods. I'd position it as something unique and interesting to non-Jews."

Jenn attended New Rochelle High School, and that's when her eyes opened to the diverse community around her. It was then that Jenn also realized how lucky she had been during the first 14 years of her life. She learned that some of her classmates' families couldn't afford to put three meals a day on the table. She realized that most of her classmates didn't hire tutors like her parents did to ensure that Jenn's grades were always near the top of her class. Jenn paid attention to the fact that after school, she had the time and opportunity to get involved with extracurricular activities while many of her classmates needed to work after-school jobs to help their families pay the bills.

In high school, Jenn was an active member of the theater and chorus groups, and developed great confidence through those activities, learning how to speak her mind and be brave with her words. Jenn's hard work paid off. She graduated valedictorian of her high school and earned a spot at Harvard University.

Jenn's First Jobs

When Jenn stepped onto the Harvard University campus, she had her life plan pretty much laid out. Attend a good college, work at a respectable company for four years, then attend a good business school just as her parents both had. But while Jenn had big dreams for her career, she wasn't exactly sure what those dreams were quite yet.

After graduating Harvard University, Jenn did indeed get a good job at a company called Starwood. Located in New York City, Starwood manages hotels all over the world. While there, Jenn was quick to raise her hand in meetings, speak her mind, share her opinions, and even point out other people's flaws. She considered her work ethic one of her most positive and ambitious characteristics about being a woman in the business world. But one day, Jenn's viewpoint and character were momentarily shattered.

After leaving a meeting where she had, once again, spoken up and shared her thoughts, Jenn's boss—a woman about 15 years older than she—pulled Jenn aside. The boss asked Jenn to sit down so she could share some "advice" for advancing her business career. Jenn eagerly took a seat but couldn't believe what she heard. "You need to shut up," her boss bluntly stated. "You're a girl. It's more becoming if you acted sweet in conversations. You're too confident. Too bold. And it's coming across the wrong way."

Jenn's boss left and Jenn broke down in tears, completely devasted. A senior executive saw that Jenn was upset. He asked her what was wrong and when Jenn explained what had just happened, the executive looked her in the eye and said, "Jenn, you keep doing what you're doing because that woman is going to work for you some day. Just act like yourself." Those encouraging words did the trick. Jenn picked herself up and never looked back. She never stopped believing in her ideas or her hard work ethic.

After four years of working at Starwood, Jenn was accepted into Harvard Business School, just as she had planned. And on the first day, she met a classmate name Jennifer Fleiss. Jenny, as she likes to be called, grew up in New York City and had attended Yale University. Jenn and Jenny became fast friends.

What Is Business School?

Business school is a graduate program where young adults go to earn a master of business administration, or MBA. Most MBA students attend business school after working a few years in the real world. MBA programs are typically two years for full-time students and four years for part-time students. At business school, students learn about many of the different facets of business, including finance, strategy, accounting, marketing, entrepreneurship, nonprofits, and leadership.

The Idea

During Jenn's second year, she went home over Thanksgiving break to visit her family. Jenn's younger sister, Becky, pulled out a beautiful designer dress from her closet. Becky had recently purchased it to wear at an upcoming friend's wedding. Jenn looked at the price tag and gasped. The extravagant dress cost more than Becky's monthly rent and had sent her sister into credit card debt. Jenn couldn't understand why Becky would be so financially irresponsible and asked why she didn't just wear a dress that she already owned.

"I can't wear them again," Becky explained. "I've worn them before and the photos are up on social media." At first, this baffled Jenn. Her sister was just a regular person, not a celebrity or public figure. Why would she care if someone saw her in the same dress twice? But then Jenn considered how regular people like Becky had a following on social media and felt like they couldn't be photographed in the same outfit twice. Jenn thought to herself, *There has to be a better solution.*

Jenn racked her brain that weekend about what problem Becky and people like her struggled with. Designer dresses were expensive, but women wanted to wear new clothes each time they went out in public. She also recognized that Becky didn't actually care about owning the dress. She cared about the *experience* of owning the dress. That meant Becky wanted to be seen, photographed, and posted on social media in something new every time she went out. Jenn thought about how to solve this problem and wondered, *Would women be interested in* renting *designer dresses?*

Renting vs. Buying

Over the past decade, the world has moved from a buying economy to a renting economy, and Rent the Runway was one of the pioneers. Even before Uber or Airbnb, Jenn Hyman thought renting, not owning, was the way to go. There are many things that make sense to rent instead of buy, including movies, cars, and vacation homes.

After Thanksgiving weekend was over, Jenn went back to Harvard Business School and asked Jenny to have lunch to hear her new idea. Jenny listened carefully as Jenn explained an idea for a rental dress company. When Jenn finished, Jenny thought for a moment and responded, "Oh, that sounds fun. Let's work on this idea. Who should we call?"

"Diane von Furstenberg," Jenn answered. Neither Jenn nor Jenny knew Diane nor had her contact information, but they thought they might be able to figure out her email address. They drafted an email and sent it to more than a dozen different versions of Diane's email at her company. Finally, one didn't bounce back. In their email, Jenn and Jenny explained a business idea for a rental dress company and asked for a meeting. Diane wrote back, "I'll see you tomorrow at 5:00 PM."

Jenn and Jenny jumped in their car the next day and headed to New York City. They didn't have a business plan, only an idea and natural fearlessness. Worst case, they figured, they would make some mistakes and learn from them. "I think people waste so much time strategizing about what they should do, rather than just going and doing something, making mistakes, and then pivoting," Jenn explained. "The goal of a startup should be: Launch as many things as possible, fail as quickly as possible, and then figure out how to move forward from there."

The two young women entered Diane von Furstenberg's office. They wore Diane's dresses and introduced themselves as the founders of Rent the Runway—a name they invented on the spot! Jenn and Jenny shared their idea, the problem, and their solution.

The problem was that women, young women in particular, couldn't afford new designer dresses, but they wanted to be seen in new clothes each time they went out. Rent the Runway would solve this problem by allowing young women to rent Diane von Furstenberg's dresses through the internet.

Diane listened carefully. She liked how Rent the Runway focused on women in their teens, twenties, and thirties. Diane's consumers were mostly older women in their fifties and sixties, and she was intrigued with the opportunity to reach younger women.

But Diane didn't like some aspects of their idea. She didn't want to be the only designer involved, and thought that if Rent the Runway could sign on multiple designers, she might be interested. She told Jenn and Jenny to come back in a few weeks after they figured out how to make Rent the Runway a company with several designers. Diane's suggestion turned out to be pivotal. The famous designer passed along a few contacts and wished them good luck.

Jenn and Jenny spent the next several weeks calling designers and getting them on board with the idea. Next, they needed to test out their idea and see if women really would rent a designer dress for a fraction of the price to buy it. They created a test store. Jenn and Jenny pooled their own money and purchased a wardrobe full of designer dresses, making sure the dresses were in their sizes. They figured that if their idea failed, at least they would both have a closet full of gorgeous dresses.

With the help of Jenn's sister Becky, the three women set up a pop-up dress shop on Harvard's campus. They hung the dresses on racks, laid out full-length mirrors, and opened Rent the Runway for college and graduate students to browse and rent. Women came from across campus to touch, see, and try on the dresses.

The response was tremendous. Jenn remembered one woman excitedly throwing on a Tory Burch sequined dress and shouting, "I look so hot!" Jenn and Jenny turned to each other and smiled, knowing their idea was not just good—it was revolutionary.

The two women hustled over the next several weeks, pulling together a website, hosting photo shoots with models in their dresses, raising money so they could purchase dresses in different sizes, and adding more designers like Hervé Léger, Catherine Malandrino, and Proenza Schouler to their portfolio. Before long, Jenn and Jenny realized that Rent the Runway was much more than a fashion company—it was also a technology company. And since neither woman had a technology background, they scrambled to hire a tech department.

Weeks later, Jenn and Jenny's long hours and fierce determination paid off. It was launch day! And as luck would have it, the *New York Times* ran a cover story on the two Harvard Business School friends and their entrepreneurial journey to opening day. The newspaper snapped photos of the women in their warehouse with racks of designer dresses. Rent the Runway launched, the *New York Times* article hit, and 100,000 women signed up in its first days.

To grow Rent the Runway's business, Jenn and Jenny needed to understand what women wanted in their dresses. They asked themselves questions: *Were women renting more short dresses or long? Were they renting more black dresses or colored? Was a certain material more popular than others? Which days of the week were most desired? Which designers were most popular and stayed popular? Which designers were trendy for a short period of time, then fizzled* out? *Which holidays created a spike in orders and which ones barely changed demand?*

They also struggled with logistics, distribution, dry cleaning, and website questions. They worked hard answering new questions: *What's the best way to mail a dress in time for a Friday- or Saturday-night party? How fast could they get a dress back, dry cleaned, and shipped out for the next weekend? Should Rent the Runway use UPS, FedEx, or USPS? How many days should the rental period be? Should Rent the Runway charge different prices for different dresses? Should they charge more for more popular styles? Should they charge more for more popular days of the week or holidays?*

Ellen Eglin, Inventor of the Clothes Wringer

Ellen was born in 1849, and back then, clothes were washed by hand, twisted, and pounded until they were wrung clean. Ellen created the clothes wringer, which allowed users to wind a crank to squeeze the clothes through parallel rollers, where the dirty water came out. Unfortunately, Ellen never saw the fame from her invention. She lived in racist times, and believed that if people knew she was Black, they wouldn't want to buy her product. Instead, she sold her invention to a patent agent for just $18.

To answer these questions, Jenn and Jenny created an analytics team that used the data from their customers' orders to figure out trends:

Analytics gets involved in all of our website metrics, thinking through where people click on the site, what email campaigns are working and which methods of traffic are working. They get involved in projecting out future trends in doing a personalization engine: because you expressed interest and clicked on this dress, you're going to like these dresses. The analytics group is working on a fit engine to really evolve the fit instructions that we give to women. They're also working on a pricing engine to really optimize the pricing and the structure of what we do.

Rent the Runway launched with designer dresses, then quickly expanded into other types of clothing and accessories. But Jenn started to notice a "problem" with their business plan: women enjoyed renting a dress once in a while, like for a special occasion or holiday, but there wasn't any *recurring revenue* coming into the company. The founders needed to figure out how to create a business model where customers were renting clothes all the time.

To solve this problem, Jenn and Jenny launched a subscription service called Rent the Runway Unlimited. Each month customers paid a certain amount and could pick out multiple items of clothes, changing it up each month. This turned out to be an especially good clothing solution for professional working women as they could rent beautiful coats, designer suits, and jewelry, and often get four pieces for the price of one. Jenn explained, "Seventy-five million professional women in this country spend three thousand dollars a year or more on clothing for work, and they're getting three thousand dollars' worth of value. Our subscribers spend nineteen hundred dollars a year, and last year the average subscriber got forty thousand dollars' worth of value."

Clothing Fact: The average American buys 68 items of clothing a year, 80 percent of which are seldom worn and 50 percent are worn not worn more than three times. Twenty percent of what the $2.4 trillion global fashion industry generates is thrown away.

Jenn Hyman and Rent the Runway Today

Today, Rent the Runway has customers across the globe, including high-profile fans such as TV news anchors, Broadway performers, and politicians. The company was valued at $1 billion in 2020 (before COVID), a milestone achieved by fewer than 20 women in the United States. Jenn Hyman has truly transformed the fashion industry.

Jenn was once asked if she rents her clothes from Rent the Runway. She answered, "I rent everything in my life except my pajamas, my undergarments, and my shoes." Jenn has truly become a pioneer in shifting the world from owning things to renting them. But her greatest joy comes from hearing that women use Rent the Runway to feel the way they have always wanted to feel through clothes, whether it is beautiful, sexy, powerful, or bold. And they do it in a financially responsible way by renting them.

Sarah Boone, Inventor of the Ironing Board

Sarah was born into slavery in 1832, but later in life moved to New Haven, Connecticut, with her husband and eight children. There she became a dressmaker and invented an ironing board that was wide enough to fit women's dresses, and narrow at the top to slip the sleeve of a shirt through. Sarah was granted a patent for her invention in 1892, becoming one of the first African American women to do so.

Follow Jenn Hyman and Rent the Runway Online:

Website: www.renttherunway.com

Instagram: @renttherunway

Twitter: @Jenn_RTR and @RenttheRunway

Facebook: Rent The Runway

Sara Blakely: Spanx

Sara Blakely clutched her "lucky" red backpack and took a deep breath to calm her nerves. In it was a Ziploc bag that held Sara's one and only prototype for an undergarment she had invented. She called it Spanx, and it made women look and feel fabulous in their clothes. Sara's heart pounded nervously as she recognized the importance of the meeting she was about to enter. It was with the buyer from Neiman Marcus who could literally change her life by placing an order. The door opened briskly, and a perfectly dressed woman greeted her and asked Sara to come in. What Sara did next would change her life, and create an entire new category of clothing for women.

Born on February 27, 1971, Sara Blakely grew up in Clearwater, Florida. Each night, her father, an injury lawyer, asked Sara and her brother Ford, "So, what did you fail at today?" It was a simple question that engrained an important message in Sara's mind. failing was not only OK; but also it was important. Failing, her father explained, allowed a person an opportunity to learn and grow.

Sara had a happy childhood, always smiling and coming up with clever ways to make a buck, like charging neighborhood kids to walk through her homemade haunted house. Sara was a high school cheerleader and a member of the debate team. But when Sara was 16, the tall, young blond witnessed one of the worst things imaginable, and it momentarily wiped the smile from her face. One day, a car hit and killed her best friend, right in front of Sara. "I think that when you witness death at age 16, there's a sense of urgency about life," she explained.

The year got harder. A few months later, Sara's mother and father separated from each other, and the tragedies didn't stop there. Soon, Sara's high school prom dates from her junior and her senior years died in separate tragic accidents.

Needless to say, times were very hard, and Sara struggled to find that wide, toothy smile that had lit up the room during most of her childhood. Sara borrowed some motivational tapes that her father used for business, hoping they could help. She listened to them over and over on her cassette player. Over time, they taught her how to find good, even in the toughest of times, and, more important, to never give up hope. "Some people would call that time in my life a string of failures," Sara explained. "But I believe that failure, in essence, is just life's way of nudging you and letting you know you're off course."

Sara's First Jobs

Sara embraced her newfound positive way of thinking and started to look for opportunities to earn money. She noticed that the beach near her home was always filled with vacationing families. Kids wanted to play in the sun, but their parents didn't always have the energy to keep up for several hours. So, she created her first business: a babysitting club outside the Clearwater Beach Hilton. Sara charged eight dollars a child and watched young kids as their parents sunbathed, walked on the beach, or relaxed by the pool. Sara's summer gig operated for three summers until the Hilton hotel manager discovered what she was doing and escorted Sara off the property.

After college, Sara turned her sights to law school. Sara knew that to get into law school, she must pass the LSAT exam. She spent months studying for the famously hard test. And failed. So, she took it again. And she failed again. In fact, her LSAT test scores were so bad that Sara dumped her dreams of law school and drove to Orlando, Florida, to audition as Goofy, her favorite clumsy character, at Walt Disney World. And although Sara learned she was too short to play Goofy, she accepted a job of buckling seat belts on riders at Epcot.

Three months later, it was clear that Walt Disney World seat-belt buckling was not Sara's magical dream job. Sara was an outgoing, charismatic person and was naturally drawn to sales, so she took a job selling fax machines for a company called Danka: "They gave me a cubicle, a phone book, and a territory of four zip codes in Clearwater and said, 'Now go sell $20,000 of fax machines a month door-to-door.'" While not an easy job, Sara was good at it and by 25, she was promoted to sales manager.

Sara learned that selling fax machines door-to-door, combined with the hot Florida sun and the pantyhose she wore underneath her business suits, left her slightly miserable. The pantyhose were restricting, uncomfortable, and unnecessarily hot, while the unattractive toes stuck out from sandals and heels. But Sara *did* like the way the control-top portion around her belly made her clothes fit better and didn't show the lines of her underwear in skirts or pants.

The Idea

One evening while Sara was dressing for a party, she pulled a beautiful pair of cream-colored pants from her closet. They had cost $98. Despite them being one of her favorites and costing so much money, Sara rarely wore these pants because she didn't like the way her bum looked in them. On a whim, Sara grabbed a pair of control-top pantyhose, impulsively reached for a pair of scissors, and started cutting. She snipped off the feet of her pantyhose, leaving just the legs and control top. She pulled them on first, then her cream-colored pants, and an idea was born. Sara looked amazing! Her bum, her tummy, her legs—all fit better under her favorite cream-colored pants. Sara smiled and left for the party. That night, one thought wouldn't leave her mind: "This should exist for women."

Sara didn't know anything about fashion. She didn't know anything about starting a business. She had never worked in retail and had only recently moved out of her mom's house. But she had $5,000 in savings and a determination to figure it out how to make this idea work.

When Sara was 27, she moved to Atlanta, Georgia and continued to sell fax machines during the day. In the evenings, she went to the Georgia Tech library to research how and where hosiery was made. It turned out that the bulk of hosiery was made in North Carolina. For months she called the managers of hosiery factories, explaining that she had a created a new type of hosiery to be worn under clothing. But repeatedly, all she heard on the other end of the phone was "No." Sara tried to explain to these managers (all of whom were men) that women wanted a product like this. She also didn't understand how people who didn't even wear pantyhose ran the pantyhose factories and made the decisions on what women should be wearing. It didn't make sense!

After months of rejections, Sara took a week off from work. During that week, she drove from Atlanta to North Carolina to meet the managers in person. She knew that if she could just show them her drawings and explain in person the idea for her new type of undergarment, they would want to partner with her. However, much to her dismay, they all said no . . . again!

Two weeks later, the phone rang. A manager from Highland Mills in Asheboro, North Carolina, asked to speak to Sara. In a thick Southern accent, he said, "Sara, I have decided to help you make your crazy idea." His name was Sam. Sam explained that he had shared her undergarment idea with his three daughters, and they thought it was brilliant. He agreed to manufacture Sara's product.

Sara needed to protect her idea with a patent, the government's protection for an invention. But the legal fees would run her close to $5,000, so instead of paying a lawyer to file the patent, Sara bought a "How to make a patent" textbook from her local bookstore.

While working on the patent, Sara considered dozens of names for her company, but she thought they were all terrible. At one point, the front-runner was Ophelia's Open Toes. Sara tried to recall the tips she had read about what makes a good name for a company, and remembered reading that having a "K" sound in the name made it memorable. In addition, she knew comedians used the K sound to make people laugh. She liked that! Inspired by the names Coca-Cola and Kodak, which at the time were the two most recognizable names in the world, Sara racked her brain for K-sounding words, but came up empty.

Then one day while sitting in traffic, it came to her—Spanks! The name Spanks made her laugh because spanking had to do with one's derriere, and her products were also about one's rear end! Sara also remembered reading that made-up names often sold better and were easier to trademark, so she changed the "ks" to an "x"—and "Spanx" was born!

What Is a Patent?

According to the United States Patent and Trademark Office, there are three types of patents:

Utility patents may be granted to anyone who invents or discovers any new and useful process, machine, article of manufacture, or composition of matter, or any new and useful improvement thereof;

Design patents may be granted to anyone who invents a new, original, and ornamental design for an article of manufacture; and

Plant patents may be granted to anyone who invents or discovers and asexually reproduces any distinct and new variety of plant.

How Do You File for a Patent?

The best place to start is the United States Patent and Trademark Office online. Here, they explain that "the United States Patent and Trademark Office (USPTO or Office) is an agency of the US Department of Commerce. The role of the USPTO is to grant patents for the protection of inventions and to register trademarks." This website walks inventors through all the steps of how to protect their inventions.

Sara met with Sam and the members of his hosiery factory and learned several things about how hosiery was made. One, factories made the same size waistband for all hosiery, no matter if the woman was petite or large. Two, they included a cord in the waistband, which often cut the circulation around a woman's waist. Neither of these design elements made sense to Sara. She insisted that Spanx be uniquely shaped for each woman's size and that all the cords be removed from the waistbands.

Next, she worked on the fabric. It had to be high quality, durable, and perfectly shaped to hold a woman's body under her clothes. Then came packaging. In the evenings after work, Sara drove to a friend's apartment and together they worked on the packaging design. Her friend was a graphic artist, and together they created a package that featured a blond cartoon character with a high ponytail who proudly wore the Spanx undergarment.

Marion Donovan, Inventor of Disposable Diapers

Marion Donovan was determined to solve the problem of diapers. When cloth diapers were the only option, she used shower curtains to create a waterproof cover for diapers and sold them directly to Saks Fifth Avenue. After selling her patent for this design for millions of dollars, she next invented the disposable diaper with a material that pulled moisture away from the baby's skin and kept him or her dry. Her invention eventually led to the creation of Pampers.

Sara wasn't quite sure what else should go on her packaging, so she went to a local department store and purchased a package of every competitor's product she could find. She laid them on the ground and studied them, searching for common information that appeared on each package. Sara copied the basic information about size recommendations and noticed that they all had the same legal jargon on their package. She figured she could save herself the legal fees and copied it, putting the exact same wording on Spanx's packaging.

With a product, patent, and packaging in hand, Sara now needed to get Spanx into stores. She picked up the phone and called her local Neiman Marcus and asked if she could show them her invention. Little did Sara know that everything sold within a department store was decided by the buyers who work at the department store's headquarters. Neiman Marcus's headquarters were in Dallas, Texas, so Sara picked up the phone and called them. No one answered for days. Then one day, the buyer picked up! Sara quickly and excitedly explained, "Hi, my name is Sara Blakely, and I've invented a product that will absolutely change the way every single one of your customers wear clothes. I just need ten minutes of your time." The buyer agreed to give her 10 minutes. Sara jumped on a plane and flew to Dallas, Texas.

Armed with her Spanx prototype, or first model of the invention, which was safely sealed in a Ziploc bag, and a color printout of the Spanx packaging, Sara nervously stepped into the buyer's office. An impeccably dressed woman greeted her. Sara shakily pulled the Spanx Ziploc from her beat-up "lucky" red backpack and started the presentation. The buyer looked on with minimal interest, and that's when Sara stopped midsentence. She looked at the buyer directly in the eyes and asked, "Will you come with me to the bathroom so I can show you a before and after of my product?"

The buyer paused for a second with a startled look as if to say, *Why would I follow a stranger into a bathroom?* But much to Sara's delight, the woman agreed. And a moment later, her mouth dropped open as she gawked at Sara's new figure, now with a pair of Spanx on. "Wow," the buyer said. "I get it. It's brilliant." She would give Spanx a shot at success, purchasing enough product to put in seven stores.

Sell-In vs. Sell-Thru

Sell-in is selling a product into a store that will ultimately sell your product to the customers. **Sell-thru** is having customers walk into that store (or go online) and purchase your product.

Thrilled with the order, Sara now needed customers to walk into Neiman Marcus and buy her product. No one had ever heard of Spanx or knew what they did, so where would customers come from? But like usual, Sara had an idea: she picked up the phone and called every person she knew in the geographical areas of the seven Neiman Marcus stores and asked them to do her a favor. She asked, "Do you mind going to the store and buying Spanx and I'll send you a check?" Sara promised to reimburse all Spanx purchases with her own money.

For weeks, Sara called people she knew, or sort of knew, sent checks, and created her own hype. It was a little sneaky, but it worked. Department stores paid attention and ordered more Spanx. With Neiman's blessing in the bag, Sara convinced Bloomingdale's, Saks, and Bergdorf Goodman to put Spanx into their stores.

Growing It

With no money for marketing or public relations (PR), Sara relentlessly put Spanx in the hands of influential people. She sent free samples to journalists at magazines, newspapers, and television shows, but her big break came from Oprah Winfrey. In the fall of 2000, Sara sent samples to Oprah's hairdresser Andre Walker, and days later noticed Oprah looked great on TV. Then one day, Oprah's people called. Oprah had picked Spanx as her Favorite Thing of 2000. *The Oprah Winfrey Show* was coming to Atlanta, Georgia, to film Sara and told her to get her website ready for a massive number of orders.

Sara quit her fax sales job two weeks before Oprah's Favorite Things show aired in November 2000 and never looked back. After Oprah's show ran, Sara's sales exploded! Spanx sold $4 million its first year. Plus, she had created an entirely new category of women's clothing called Shapewear. Sara understood the importance of this lucky break and didn't let it fade away. Instead, she took advantage of the moment: "A lot of entrepreneurs make the mistake of sitting back. I was going to ensure my own success."

It wasn't easy. For the next two years, Sara traveled the country, visiting department store after department store. She held morning meetings with the salespeople on the floor, explaining what Spanx were, modeling her own booty in them, and having other women model their bottoms as well. Then, for hours, Sara stood near the entranceway and talked to customers as they rolled in. She explained what her product was and how it worked.

Salespeople and customers immediately loved Spanx once they were educated, but Sara quickly recognized she had another problem. Her product was hard to find among the dozens of hosiery brands at department stores. The chances of a customer pulling out Sara's one and only product out of a wall of dozens of products was very low. Plus, Sara didn't believe Spanx was even a hosiery product. Women would buy it when they were dressing for something special like a party, wedding, or holiday. Spanx needed to be near designer handbags and heels!

So, Sara got creative again. She drove to Target and purchased small silver display cases from the office supply aisle, then walked confidently into Neiman Marcus stores, plucked her Spanx products from the wall of hosiery, and set up Spanx displays near cash registers, handbags, and heels. It worked! Soon the salespeople from the dress department wanted them on their floor because Spanx also helped sell other clothes. The department store salespeople pushed Spanx on their customers, knowing that they looked better in most clothes with them on. Suddenly, Sara had created an enormous sales force without having to pay a single person!

Sales of Spanx continued to grow. The media also fell in love with Sara and her entrepreneurial story. *Forbes* magazine ran a story that proclaimed Sara as an "accidental entrepreneur" who had reinvented the girdle. In 2001, Sara appeared on QVC, the television shopping channel. They gave her five minutes to explain the product. Sara sold 8,000 pairs of Spanx in five minutes!

By the end of her second year, sales hit $10 million. Oprah continued to rave about Spanx year after year, and the famous talk show host became Sara's luckiest charm. With Oprah's repeated blessing, Spanx continued to grow with more styles, more colors, and more sales. By 2006 Spanx had over $100 million in sales.

Oprah Winfrey

Oprah Winfrey is best known for being an American talk show host of *The Oprah Winfrey Show* from 1986 to 2001. It was the highest-rated talk show program in history, and Oprah expanded her brand to magazines, television, and philanthropic programs. And while Oprah grew up in poverty in Mississippi, she became very successful, ultimately claiming the title of the wealthiest African American of the 20th century and the first Black multibillionaire.

Sara Blakely and Spanx Today

Spanx's success story is quite remarkable. The company is a private company, which means its financial information is kept private. This differs from a public company, which has shareholders and financial information must be released each year in an annual report. Despite not knowing exactly what Spanx's sales are, here's what is known about Sara's wealth. Sara owns 100 percent of Spanx, has no debt, and no investment partners. In 2013 Sara Blakely signed the Melinda and Bill Gates's and Warren Buffett's Giving Pledge, which promises that the individual will give at least half her wealth to charity. In 2017 Sara Blakely became the youngest self-made billionaire in the world, an accomplishment that as of 2021, only eight women have achieved. Sara's extraordinary success makes her part of a very small group of women who are billionaires without the help of a husband or inheritance. Another influential woman who is part of this elite group: Oprah Winfrey—Sara's lucky charm!

Sara also gives back each year to women who have the same entrepreneurial drive she has. She founded the Sara Blakely Foundation, which supports and empowers underserved women and girls. To date, Sara has donated $17.5 million to this foundation, and the money is used to provide college scholarships, homes for single mothers, and empowerment grants.

Sara continues to amaze the world with her charm, her humor, and her great big smile. And looking back on her journey, she explained, "Since I was a little girl, I have always known I would help women. In my wildest dreams I never thought I would have started with their butts. As it turns out, that was a great place to start!"

Follow Sara Blakely and Spanx Online:

Website: www.spanx.com

Instagram: @SaraBlakely and @spanx

Twitter: @SPANX

Facebook: SPANX

Afterword

What's YOUR Big Idea?

Stop for a moment and look around you. The shoes on your feet, the clothes on your body, the computer on your desk, the toys you play with, the soap you wash with, the car you drive in, and even this book were all just an idea once. Science tells us that we have around 6,000 thoughts in one day, and many of these thoughts are ideas for something new and innovative. And while most thoughts and ideas pop in our heads and disappear moments later, some ideas won't leave. These are the ideas you should pay attention to. These are the ideas that could change the world.

Ideas come from many different places. Some ideas come from *solving a problem* like **Heidi Zak** and her idea to develop a better bra and better bra shopping experience for girls, teenagers, and women. **Jenn Hyman**'s idea also solved a problem - it gave women a way to rent designer clothes at affordable prices, rather than buy them. **Anne Wojiciki** wanted to solve a problem in the health care industry by empowering people with their DNA information.

Sometimes ideas come from *one's passion*. **Alli Webb**'s passion for blowing out and styling women's hair turned into a revolutionary new concept for a hair salon business. **Payal Kadakia** loved to dance more than anything and used her analytical brain to figure out a way to combine her passion for dance into a business. And **Lisa Price** turned her passion for creating scented oils and beauty products into a thriving company.

Sometimes ideas come from a desire to **help others**. Consider **Reshma Saujani** who powered through two careers before she succeeded at her mission in life to help others by teaching girls to code. **Jasmine Crowe** also created a business based around her desire to help others and now feeds hundreds of thousands of food-insecure individuals while also helping to reduce food waste and improve the environment.

While it's not as common, sometimes an idea can hit like a bolt of lightning, like the way **Sara Blakely** thought of her idea for a different type of women's undergarment.

And finally, many good ideas *evolve naturally from hard work, determination, and competitiveness*. **Kathleen King** and **Christina Tosi** both proved that even when life gets hard, entrepreneurship can be the answer in the food business. And **Stacy Madison's** love for food gradually evolved into an innovative and thriving pita chip business.

The goal of this book is to introduce you to the true stories behind some of the world's most incredible female entrepreneurs. They come from various backgrounds, different ethnicities, and a wide range of educational levels but prove they have one thing in common: these women combined their *idea* with *hard work* and *passion* to create a business that changed the world.

So what's next for you? Maybe your idea will hit you in one year, five years, or even twenty years from now. Be patient and stay tuned into your thoughts and observations.

If you are one of the few kids with an idea now, I encourage you to enter my **Kids Idea Tank** competition, the largest entrepreneurship competition for kids age 8 through 13. Finalists at Kids Idea Tank pitch their idea to a panel of judges for a chance to win huge prize money and even talk to some of the fearless female entrepreneurs featured in this book!

Good luck and Think Big Ideas!

Lowey

Follow Lowey Bundy Sichol and Kids Idea Tank Online:

Website: www.LoweyBundySichol.com

Instagram: @LoweySichol and @IdeaTank4Kids

Twitter: @LoweySichol

Acknowledgments

Idea Makers was written during the COVID-19 pandemic. That meant my usual writing spot at the local library was shut down and my quiet home office was suddenly surrounded by Zooms for school, homework help, frisbee boredom breaks, and endless pleas for snacks. But throughout that time, my family also acknowledged the importance of this book, and when my office door closed, *Idea Makers* came to life. Thank you to my husband, Adam, and my three children Carter, Peyton, and Tucker for their love and support.

Next, I want to thank the fifteen female entrepreneurs featured in this book for their innovative ideas and, of course, for their fearlessness. It is my honor to share *your* stories to the next generation in hopes of inspiring them to change the world with *their* ideas.

Specifically, I would like to thank the seven women who took time out of their busy schedules to talk with me in depth about their lives and journey as an entrepreneur: Stacy Madison, Alli Webb, Reshma Saujani, Payal Kadakia, Kathleen King, Heidi Zak, and Cindy Oh Lin. I am beyond grateful for the time you spent with me

Acknowledgments

Thank you to my incredible agent Elizabeth Bennett, who listens patiently to my crazy ideas for children's books about entrepreneurship and business and handpicks the best like the pro she is and always has been.

Thank you to my editors, Jerry Pohlen and Ben Krapohl, for your wisdom, promptness, and perfect grammar.

Thank you to all the librarians and teachers who support my passion for introducing entrepreneurship to kids. You are my heroes.

Thank you to my goofy and sweet dogs, Commodore and Captain, who sit patiently at my feet, providing companionship during a solitary profession.

Finally, thank you to all the entrepreneurs who risk everything to follow their dreams and change our world with their ideas. Entrepreneurs come from all backgrounds, ethnicities, and genders, but their stories too often go untold, especially to children. Kids need to know that entrepreneurs can look like them, think like them, and come from the same background as them. Only then will kids know that anything is possible.

Think big ideas and be fearless!

Notes

Introduction

Today, there are more: Ventureneer with CoreWomen, "The 2019 State of Women-Owned Businesses Report," American Express, accessed July 26, 2021, https://s1.q4cdn.com/692158879/files/ doc_library/file/2019-state-of-women-owned-businesses-report.pdf.

Chapter 1: Kathleen King—Tate's Bake Shop

"I wonder why": All quotations from original author interviews with Kathleen King on July 8, 2020, and May 4, 2021, unless otherwise noted here.

"I had the gift of": "Tate's Bake Shop: Kathleen King," *How I Built This with Guy Raz*, December 16, 2019, www.npr .org/2019/12/13/787897696/tates-bake-shop-kathleen-king.

In 2020 the Washington Post: Matt Brooks, "Who Makes the Best

Chocolate Chip Cookie? We Tasted 14 Top Brands and Ranked Them," www.washingtonpost.com/food/2020/12/04/best-chocolate-chip-cookie-brands/.

Chapter 2: Stacy Madison—Stacy's Pita Chips

"This was the best thing": All quotations from original author interview with Stacy Madison on January 21, 2021, unless otherwise noted here.

"We were basically making toast": Guy Raz, "Stacy's Pita Chips: Stacy Madison," May 27, 2019, on *How I Built This with Guy Raz*, NPR, podcast, 1:05:54, https://www.npr.org/2019/05/24/726755480/stacys-pita-chips-stacy-madison.

"Holy cow!": Raz, "Stacy's Pita Chips: Stacy Madison," *How I Built This*.

Florence Parpart was born: Morgan Rees, "Florence Parpart – Patented the Modern Refrigerator," Women's Suite, accessed July 20, 2021, https://magazine.womenssuite.com/florence-parpart-patented-the-modern-refrigerator/.

"We built our business": Raz, "Stacy's Pita Chips: Stacy Madison," *How I Built This*.

"Hi! I'm Stacy": Raz, "Stacy's Pita Chips: Stacy Madison."

Chapter 3: Christina Tosi—Milk Bar

"Tosi don't get anything but A's": Guy Raz, "How I Built Resilience: Live with Christina Tosi and Gary Erickson & Kit Crawford," May 7, 2020, on *How I Built This with Guy Raz*, NPR, podcast, 30:13, www.npr.org/2020/05/05/850994384/how-i-built-resilience-live -with-christina-tosi-and-gary-erickson-kit-crawford.

"What is it that": Raz, "Live with Christina Tosi."

"Somehow, I was": Raz, "Live with Christina Tosi."

"I was thinking": Raz, "Live with Christina Tosi."

"Go figure out how": Raz, "Live with Christina Tosi."

"When opportunity knocks": Raz, "Live with Christina Tosi."

"Thank you very much": Natalie Robehmed, "Ina Garten on How to Run a Business and Do What You Love," *Forbes*, June 10, 2015, https://www.forbes.com/sites/natalierobehmed/2015/06/10/ina-gar-ten-on-how-to-run-a-business-and-do-what-you-love/?sh= 16cee2177535.

"our hands, not our thumbs": Raz, "Live with Christina Tosi," *How I Built This*.

Chapter 4: Lisa Price—Carol's Daughter

"He always had colorful conversation": Lisa Price, interview by Shawn Wilson with videography by Necula Burghelea, The History Makers, November 8, 2006, https://www.thehistorymakers .org/biography/lisa-price-41.

"Would you mix them for me?": Price, interview by Wilson with Burghelea.

"I figured out how": Price, interview by Wilson with Burghelea.

"What am I gonna": Price, interview by Wilson with Burghelea.

"You must have": Price, interview by Wilson with Burghelea.

"Right before Christmas": Price, interview by Wilson with Burghelea.

"We had a schedule": Price, interview by Wilson with Burghelea.

"My husband had some money": Price, interview by Wilson with Burghelea.

"appealing to": Gabi Thorne, "Iman Shared How Iman Cosmetics Has Been Promoting Diversity Since It Launched in 1994," *Allure*, June 12, 2020, https://www.allure.com/story/iman-cosmetics -diversity.

"That's the easy part": Guy Raz, "Carol's Daughter: Lisa Price,"

August 6, 2018, on *How I Built This with Guy Raz*, podcast, 43:00,
https://www.npr.org/2018/08/03/635359913/carols-daughter
-lisa-price.

Chapter 5: Payal Kadakia—ClassPass

"Only if your homework is finished": All quotations from original
author interview with Payal Kadakia on February 4, 2021, unless
otherwise noted here.

"You do this full time?": Guy Raz, "ClassPass: Paval Kadakia," June
29, 2020, on *How I Built This with Guy Raz*, podcast, 1:18:51, https://
www.npr.org/2020/06/25/883560732/classpass-payal-kadakia.

"Why don't you quit?": Raz, "ClassPass: Paval Kadakia."

"Tell me more about": Raz, "ClassPass: Paval Kadakia."

"The CEO title was" to *"I kept dancing"*: Raz, "ClassPass: Paval
Kadakia."

"I felt like I was put": "Meet Payal Kadakia, CEO and Co-Founder
of ClassPass - In Progress | Oxygen," Very Real Reality,
uploaded May 24, 2016, YouTube video, 1:34, www.youtube.com
/watch?v=2ktX8zYjSHM.

Chapter 6: Alli Webb—Drybar

"What in the world": All quotations from original author interview with Alli Webb on January 25, 2021, unless otherwise noted here.

"I have an idea" to *"Yep!"*: Kristen Aldridge, "How Drybar Founder Alli Webb Turned a Simple Concept into a $100 Million Empire," *Entrepreneur*, April 26, 2018, www.entrepreneur.com /video/311067.

"Recognize your strengths": Elana Lyn Gross, "How Alli Webb Turned Drybar into a $100M Business," *Forbes*, May 15, 2018, www .forbes.com/sites/elanagross/2018/05/15/alli-webb-drybar/?sh= 18caed4c1474#720549251474.

"The day we opened": Lindsay Blakely, "She Couldn't Stand Working with Her Brother, Then They Started a $100 Million Company Together," *Inc.*, July/August 2018, www.inc.com /magazine/201808/lindsay-blakely/how-i-did-it-alli-webb-drybar. html.

"Hell, no": Guy Raz, "Drybar: Alli Webb," July 23, 2018, on *How I Built This with Guy Raz*, NPR, podcast, 34:54, www.npr .org/2018/07/18/630168776/drybar-alli-webb.

"Don't let perfect": "Alli Webb," Tory Burch Foundation, accessed July 21, 2021, www.toryburchfoundation.org/resources/growth /alli-webb/.

"One of the biggest": "Alli Webb," Tory Burch Foundation.

Chapter 7: Anne Wojcicki—23andMe

"What are you doing?": Karlie Kloss, "ELLE X KLOSSY | Episode 1 | Anne Wojcicki Founder of 23andMe," *ELLE UK*, uploaded February 9, 2016, YouTube video, 4:30, https://www.youtube.com /watch?v=2AWxD5pIiSs.

"I would write a paper": Kevin J. Ryan, "23andMe's Anne Wojcicki Says Doing These 2 Things as a Leader Built Her Company's Culture of Honesty," *Inc.*, March/April 2019, www.inc .com/magazine/201904/kevin-j-ryan/23andme-anne-wojcicki-best -business-advice.html.

"Don't be afraid": David Silverberg, "Good Genes? The Sisters Who Put the Rest of Us to Shame," *BBC News*, December 3, 2018, www .bbc.com/news/business-46361764.

"My parents really looked": Catherine Clifford, "How Anne and Susan Wojcicki's Parents Raised the Founder of 23andMe and the CEO of YouTube," CNBC Master Class, June 18, 2018, https:// www.cnbc.com/2018/06/18/how-the-wojcickis-parents-raised -23andme-founder-youtube-ceo.html.

"It's really weird": Anne Wojcicki, "Co-Founder and CEO of 23andMe | Anne Wojcicki | Talks at Google," Talks at Google,

uploaded July 11, 2018, YouTube video, 1:03:06, www.youtube.com /watch?v=pDoALM0q1LA.

"Anne, you can either": Wojcicki, "Co-Founder and CEO of 23andMe."

"In a hand-syringe": Chris Wiltz, "10 of History's Greatest Women Inventors You Should Know," DesignNews, June 23, 2019, https://www.designnews.com/electronics-test/10 -historys-greatest-women-inventors-you-should-know /gallery?slide=5.

"You just accept": Erika Check Hayden, "The Rise, Fall and Rise Again of 23andMe," *Nature*, October 12, 2017, www.nature.com /news/polopoly_fs/1.22801!/menu/main/topColumns /topLeftColumn/pdf/550174a.pdf?origin=ppub.

"That setback": Silverberg, "Good Genes?"

"I once ate": Hayden, "Rise, Fall and Rise Again."

"People tend to look": "How 23andMe Puts Culture in Its DNA," CUtoday, May 4, 2019, http://www.cutoday.info/site/THE-corner /How-23andMe-Puts-Culture-In-Its-DNA.

Chapter 8: Morgan DeBaun—Blavity

"We had Black Santas": Keryce Chelsi Henry, "Morgan DeBaun Is

Putting Black Millennials' Voices Center Stage," *Nylon*, February 27, 2016, www.nylon.com/articles/morgan-debaun-interview.

"The first week": Henry, "Morgan DeBaun."

"I found myself thinking": John Ketchum, "Blavity's CEO on Taking Risks and Building a Community for Black Millennials," *CNN Business*, April 20, 2017, https://money.cnn.com/2017/04/20/technology/morgan-debaun-blavity/index.html.

"So, I'm sitting" to *"And so at that moment"*: Kelsea Stahler, "How 'Blavity' Co-Founder Morgan DeBraun Became One of the Most Important Women in Silicon Valley," *Bustle*, August 16, 2018, https://www.bustle.com/p/how-blavity-co-founder-morgan-debaun-became-one-of-the-most-important-women-in-silicon-valley-10133055.

"#BlackLivesMatter": "Black Lives Matter: About," Black Lives Matter, accessed July 22, 2021, https://blacklivesmatter.com/about/.

"You have to remember": Kevin Stankiewicz, "Black Founders Receiving More Venture Capital Spurs Innovation, Says Entrepreneur Morgan DeBaun," CNBC, September 10, 2020, www.cnbc.com/2020/09/10/blavity-ceo-morgan-debaun-on-black-founders-receiving-more-vc-funding.html.

"I'm from the Midwest": Stankiewicz, "Black Founders Receiving More Venture Capital."

"One of the specific stories": Stahler, "How 'Blavity' Co-Founder."

"I'll be honest with you": Stahler.

Chapter 9: Jasmine Crowe—Goodr

What on earth: Jasmine Crowe, "What We're Getting Wrong in the Fight to End Hunger," TEDWomen 2019, December 2019, www.ted.com/talks/jasmine_crowe_what_we_re_getting_wrong_in_the_fight_to_end_hunger#t-6562.

"I definitely have": Jasmine Crowe, "Beyond the Bio: Jasmine Crowe," TEDxPeachtree, August 14, 2017, http://tedxpeachtree.com/beyond-bio-jasmine-crowe/.

"I remember the first time": Crowe, "Beyond the Bio."

"Something shook me": "Meet Jasmine Crowe of Goodr," *VoyageATL*, September 5, 2018, http://voyageatl.com/interview/meet-jasmine-crowe-goodr-nw-atlanta/.

"UberEats in reverse": Steven Gray, "Meet the Entrepreneur Disrupting the Food Industry—for Good," *Techonomy*, October 18, 2019, https://techonomy.com/2019/10/meet-the-entrepreneur

-disrupting-the-food-industry-for-good/.

"It took almost 200 meetings": "Meet Jasmine Crowe of Goodr," *VoyageATL*.

"Everyone that said": Taylor Locke, "Goodr CEO Turned Her Passion into a Multimillion-Dollar Business: 'I'm Really Motivated by All the Naysayers,'" CNBC Make It, February 19, 2021, www.cnbc.com/2021/02/19/goodr-ceo-jasmine-crowes-advice-to-build-a-successful-business.html.

"There was a lot": Locke.

Chapter 10: Sandra Oh Lin—KiwiCo

"Every year my mother": All quotes from original author interview with Sandra Oh Lin on April 16, 2021, unless otherwise noted here.

"I created hands-on": Michelle Woo, "I'm Sandra Oh Lin, Founder of KiwiCo, and This Is How I Parent," *LifeHacker*, August 13, 2018, https://offspring.lifehacker.com/im-sandra-oh-lin-founder-of-kiwico-and-this-is-how-i-1828299023.

"I was brainstorming": James F. Peltz, "Kiwi Crate CEO Sandra Oh Lin Says Starting a Business Isn't Child's Play," *Los Angeles Times*, August 6, 2015, https://www.latimes.com/business/la-fi-qa-kiwi-crate-20150806-story.html

"It is a practical demonstration": Mary Pilon, "The Secret History of Monopoly: The Capitalist Board Game's Leftwing Origins," *Guardian*, April 11, 2015, www.theguardian.com/lifeandstyle/2015/apr/11/secret-history-monopoly-capitalist-game-leftwing-origins.

"We ship out": Guy Raz, "How I Built Resilience: Sandra Oh Lin of KiwiCo," September 5, 2020, on *How I Built This with Guy Raz*, NPR, podcast, 20:29, https://www.npr.org/2020/09/03/909165521/how-i-built-resilience-sandra-oh-lin-of-kiwico.

"I recognize that": "An Interview with Sandra Oh Lin of KiwiCo & Her Advice for Female Entrepreneurs," Chip Chick, June 24, 2019, https://www.chipchick.com/2019/06/chicks-we-love-an-interview-with-sandra-oh-lin-of-kiwico-her-advice-for-female-entrepreneurs.html.

"Give kids permission": "An Interview with Sandra Oh Lin."

Chapter 11: Reshma Saujani—Girls Who Code

"dot head go home": Reshma Saujani, *Brave, Not Perfect* (New York: Currency, 2019), 113.

made up half of Apple's: Robert Johnson, "Girls Who Code CEO Seeks to Empower Women in Tech," *Cornell Chronicle*, October 8, 2015, https://news.cornell.edu/stories/2015/10/girls-who-code

-ceo-seeks-empower-women-tech.

But by 2013: Patrick Peterson, "Reshma Saujani Makes the Case for Girls Who Code," *THE Journal*, January 20, 2016, https://thejournal.com/articles/2016/01/20/reshma-saujani-makes-the-case-for-girls-who-code.aspx.

"By the end of": Reshma Saujani, "Girls Who Code Turns Five: What I've Learned Since Our Founding," *Medium*, March 22, 2017, https://medium.com/@reshmasaujani/girls-who-code-turns-five-what-ive-learned-since-our-founding-4c70861e6769.

"The demographic of": "Girls Who Code," brightest.io, www.brightest.io/cause/girls-who-code/.

"I want to give girls": Jessica Guynn, "No Boys Allowed: Girls Who Code Takes on Gender Gap," *USA Today*, August 12, 2014, www.usatoday.com/story/tech/2014/08/12/girls-who-code-facebook-sheryl-sandberg/13784445/.

Chapter 12: Cindy Mi—VIPKid

"She hated me!": Cindy Mi and Qi Lu, "On Starting and Scaling an Edtech Company in China," Y Combinator, January 16, 2019, www.ycombinator.com/library/5W-on-starting-and-scaling-an-edtech-company-in-china.

Notes

"I left the classroom": Harrison Jacobs, "A 35-Year-Old Who Dropped Out of High School Had a Vision of a Utopian Future in China, the US, and the World—and It's Led Her to the Forefront of a Tech Startup Worth $3 Billion," *Business Insider*, August 11, 2021, www.businessinsider.com/inside-vipkid-cindy-mi-and-3 -billion-startups-teacher-community-2018-8.

"Make the decision": Jacobs.

"Chinese government saw": "Education in China: A Snapshot," Organization for Economic Cooperation and Development, 2016, www.oecd.org/china/Education-in-China-a-snapshot.pdf.

"I got the privilege": Mi and Lu, "On Starting and Scaling."

"The first 18 months": Cindy Mi, "Cindy Mi on Building VIPKid, the World's Largest English Learning Platform for Children," Y Combinator, uploaded November 3, 2017, YouTube video, 33:00, www.youtube.com/watch?v=eJVTnVVJtgY.

"Teacher, come back": Mi and Lu, "On Starting and Scaling."

"It's a future": Everett Rosenfeld, "CNBC Interview with Cindy Mi, Founder & CEO, VIPKid," CNBC, November 28, 2018, https:// www.cnbc.com/2018/11/28/cnbc-interview-with-cindy-mi -founder--ceo-vipkid-.html.

"So, we were": Rosenfeld.

"What if you had": Jacobs, "A 35-Year-Old Who Dropped Out of High School."

Chapter 13: Heidi Zak—ThirdLove

"It was terrible!": All quotes from original author interview with Heidi Zak on April 30, 2021, unless otherwise noted here.

"Definitely not": "Q&A with Heidi Zak (ThirdLove)," *FORM*, Duke Arts, February 7, 2020, https://arts.duke.edu/news/qa-with -heidi-zak-thirdlove/.

"When I moved": "Q&A with Heidi Zak (ThirdLove)."

"I came out": Tariaro Mzezewa, "Victoria's Secret? In 2018, Few People Want to Hear It," *New York Times*, November 16, 2018, www.nytimes.com/2018/11/16/style/victorias-secret-bras-decline .html.

"In 2012, if you look": "Q&A with Heidi Zak (ThirdLove)," *FORM*, Duke Arts, February 7, 2020, https://arts.duke.edu/news /qa-with-heidi-zak-thirdlove/.

"I would get home": Kalika Yap, "ThirdLove Co-Founder | Heidi Zak," June 15, 2020, on *Wonder with Kalika Yap*, Apple Podcasts, podcast, 29:56, https://podcasts.apple.com/us/podcast/thirdlove -co-founder-heidi-zak/id1273127245?i=1000477966137.

"We didn't want": "Q&A with Heidi Zak (ThirdLove)," *FORM*, Duke Arts, February 7, 2020, https://arts.duke.edu/news/qa-with -heidi-zak-thirdlove/.

"We've built an inclusive brand": "Q&A with Heidi Zak (Third-Love)."

"made a list of": "Lisa Lindahl," National Inventors Hall of Fame, accessed July 22, 2021, www.invent.org/inductees/lisa-lindahl.

"If we can contribute": Nerisha Penrose, "ThirdLove Launches the TL Effect to Support Businesses Led by Women of Color," *Elle*, June 17, 2020, www.elle.com/fashion/shopping/a32892933 /thirdlove-women-of-color-tl-effect/.

Chapter 14: Jenn Hyman—Rent the Runway

"Hello?": Guy Raz, "Rent the Runway: Jenn Hyman," October 15, 2018, on *How I Built This with Guy Raz*, NPR, podcast, 56:57, www .npr.org/2018/10/12/656936877/rent-the-runway-jenn-hyman.

"It's disgusting": Emily Peck, "How Co-Founder of 'Rent the Run-way' Beat Sexism on Her Way to the Top," *HuffPost*, October 16, 2017, www.huffpost.com/entry/jennifer-hyman-rent-the -runway-business-sexism_n_59e13603e4b0a52aca181ab9.

"You need to shut up": Raz, "Rent the Runway: Jenn Hyman."

"Jenn, you keep doing": Raz.

"I can't wear them": Raz.

"Oh, that sounds fun": Raz.

"I'll see you tomorrow": Raz.

"I think people waste": Adrian Granzella Larssen, "What We've Learned: A Q&A with Rent the Runway's Founders," *Muse*, 2021, https://www.themuse.com/advice/what-weve-learned-a-qa-with -rent-the-runways-founders.

"I look so hot!": "Our Story," Rent the Runway, www .renttherunway.com/about-us/story.

"Analytics gets involved": Sasha Galbraith, "The Secret Behind Rent the Runway's Success," *Forbes*, December 3, 2013, www.forbes.com /sites/sashagalbraith/2013/12/03/the-secret-behind-rent-the -runways-success/?sh=aca36ec77e69.

"Seventy-five million": Alexandra Schwartz, "Rent the Runway Wants to Lend You Your Look, *New Yorker*, October 15, 2018, www.newyorker.com/magazine/2018/10/22/rent-the -runway-wants-to-lend-you-your-look.

The average American buys: Schwartz.

"I rent everything": Schwartz.

Sarah was born into slavery: "Sarah Boone Biography," Biography.com, updated January 13, 2021, https://www.biography .com/inventor/sarah-boone.

Chapter 15: Sara Blakely—Spanx

"I think that when you witness": "#40 Forward, Day 4: Sara Blakely, Creator of Spanx," *Lemonade Drop*, www.lemonadeday .org/blog/40forward-day-4-sarah-blakely-creator-spanx.

"Some people would call": Amy Blaschka, "Six Ways to Embrace the One Thing Sara Blakely and Gary Vaynerchuk (and My Dad) Say Is the Secret to Professional Fulfillment," *Forbes*, November 18, 2019, www.forbes.com/sites/amyblaschka/2019/11/18 /six-ways-to-embrace-the-one-thing-sara-blakely-and-gary -vaynerchuk-and-my-dad-say-is-the-secret-to-professional-fulfil lment/?sh=4c4079d419d3.

"They gave me a cubicle": Blaschka.

"This should exist for women": *Inc.* Staff, "How Spanx Got Started," *Inc.*, January 20, 2012, https://www.inc.com/sara-blakely /how-sara-blakley-started-spanx.html.

"Sara, I have decided": Guy Raz, "Spanx: Sara Blakely," June 3, 2017, on *How I Built This with Guy Raz*, NPR, podcast, 31:18, www.npr.org/2017/08/15/534771839/spanx-sara-blakely.

"Utility patents": "General Information Concerning Patents,"
United States Patent and Trademark Office, updated July 1, 2021,
https://www.uspto.gov/patents/basics/general-information-patents.

"The United States Patent": "General Information Concerning
Patents."

"Hi, my name is": *Inc.* Staff, "How She Got Spanx on Oprah,"
Inc., January 20, 2012, www.inc.com/sara-blakely/how-sara
-blakely-got-spanx-on-oprah.html.

"Will you come with me": Raz, "Spanx: Sara Blakely."

"Wow": Raz.

"Do you mind going": Raz.

"A lot of entrepreneurs": *Inc.* Staff, "How Spanx Grew," *Inc.*,
January 20, 2012, www.inc.com/sara-blakely/how-sara-blakely
-grew-spanx.html.

"Since I was a little girl": "How It All Began," About, Spanx by Sara
Blakely Foundation, www.spanxfoundation.com/about/.